Letts

GCSE
Success

Biology

**Tom
Adams**

Exam Practice Workbook

Biology

Cell Biology

Transport Systems and Photosynthesis

Health, Disease and the Development of Medicines

Coordination and Control

Contents

Inheritance, Variation and Evolution

Ecosystems

Practice Exam Papers

Answers

1 This image shows some human liver cells, as seen through a very powerful light microscope.

(a) Which organelle is labelled X? .... (1)

(b) Unlike skin cells, these cells contain many mitochondria, but they cannot be seen in the image. Suggest why not. (1)

....

(c) Why do the cells have many mitochondria? (2)

....

....

(d) Liver cells have different features.
Arrange the features in order of size, starting with the largest. (2)

gene	nucleus	cell	chromosome	cytoplasm

....

2 (a) A student is observing bacterial cells under the high power lens of a light microscope. She cannot see a nucleus in the cells and concludes that the cells do not contain DNA. Explain why this conclusion is wrong. (1)

....

....

(b) Which of the following words best describes a bacterial cell? Tick (✓) **one** box. (1)

Prokaryotic ☐

Eukaryotic ☐

Multicellular ☐

Undifferentiated ☐

For more help on this topic, see Letts GCSE Biology Revision Guide pages 4–5

1 The diagram shows a fertilised egg cell (a zygote).

(a) The zygote is described as a **stem cell**. What does this term mean? (1)

....

(b) The zygote has a very different appearance to the root hair cell (pictured right). However, all cells have some structures in common. Write down **two** of these structures. (2)

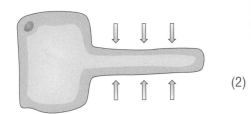

1. ....

2. ....

2 **(a)** A student attends a school trip to a medical research laboratory, where he is given a talk from a scientist on the techniques and benefits of stem cell research.

Describe **two** applications of stem cell research that the scientist is likely to mention. (2)

1. ....

2. ....

(b) After the visit, one of the student's friends says she is opposed to stem cell research. Describe **one** objection that people have to stem cell research. (1)

....

....

3 A live sperm cell is observed under the microscope beating its tail. It moves across the field of view at a rate of 200 µm every 30 seconds.

Assuming the sperm travels at the same rate and in the same direction, how far will it have travelled in one hour? Give your answer in mm. (3)

....

For more help on this topic, see Letts GCSE Biology Revision Guide pages 6–7

1 (a) Daljit is looking at some cheek cells using a light microscope under low power. He decides that he wants a more magnified view. How should he adjust the microscope?

Draw a line from X to show which part of the microscope he should adjust.

X

(1)

(b) Under higher power, Daljit clearly sees the nucleus, cytoplasm and cell membrane of the cheek cells. He would also like to see mitochondria and ribosomes. Give **two** reasons why he cannot see these structures.

(2)

....

....

(c) Using a specially fitted camera, Daljit takes a picture of the cells he sees.

He measures the diameter of one cell on his photograph by drawing a line and using a ruler. The line is shown on the picture. It measures 3 cm.

If the microscope magnifies the image 400 times, calculate the actual size of the cell in µm.

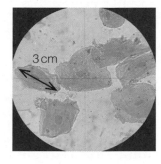
3 cm

You can use the following formula:

$$\text{magnification} = \frac{\text{size of image}}{\text{size of real object}}$$

Answer: .... µm   (3)

2 (a) Look at the photograph on the right. What type of microscope was used to take this picture?

(1)

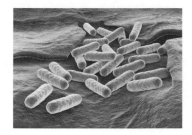

....

(b) There are 27 bacterial cells in this picture. If the bacteria have reproduced from 1 cell every 20 minutes, how long have the bacteria been growing?

(2)

.... minutes

For more help on this topic, see Letts GCSE Biology Revision Guide pages 8–9

1 The illustrations show a single-celled organism, called an amoeba, and a multicellular organism (a horse).

Not to scale

Explain why the horse has specialised organs in its breathing and digestive system, and the amoeba has none. (2)

....

....

....

....

2 Complete the following table, which compares the processes of mitosis and meiosis. (3)

Mitosis	Meiosis
Involved in asexual reproduction	....
....	Produces variation
Produces cells with 46 chromosomes	....

3 Jenny is studying chicken cells and is looking at some examples down the microscope. She draws these cells.

(a) Which type of cell division is shown here? .... (1)

(b) Give a reason for your answer to (a). (1)

....

4 Joshua wants to find out what happens to DNA molecules during cell division.

Complete the flow diagram to complete the sequence that DNA molecules go through when they replicate. (2)

Double helix 'unzips'

→

↓

←

Enzyme bonds new bases together to form complementary strands

For more help on this topic, see Letts GCSE Biology Revision Guide pages 10–11

HT **①** Isaac is running a marathon. Write a balanced symbol equation for the main type of respiration that will be occurring in his muscles. (2)

....

② Isaac's metabolic rate is monitored as part of his training schedule. He is rigged up to a metabolic rate meter. This measures the volumes of gas that he breathes in and out. The difference in these volumes represents oxygen consumption. This can be used in a calculation to show metabolic rate.

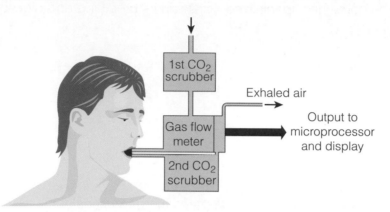

The table below shows some measurements taken from the meter over a period of one hour.

	Five minutes of jogging	Five minutes of rest	Five minutes of sprinting	Five minutes sprinting on an incline
Mean metabolic rate per ml oxygen used per kg per min	35	20	45	60

(a) The units of metabolic rate are expressed in the table as 'per kg'. Why is this adjustment made? (2)

....

....

(b) Using the table, explain the difference in readings for jogging and sprinting. (2)

....

(c) Isaac does quite a lot of exercise. His friend Boris does not. How might Boris' readings compare with Isaac's? Give a reason for your answer. (2)

....

....

For more help on this topic, see Letts GCSE Biology Revision Guide pages 12–13

1 In an experiment to investigate the enzyme catalase, potato extract was added to a solution of hydrogen peroxide. The catalase in the potato catalysed the decomposition of the hydrogen peroxide and produced oxygen bubbles. The experiment was carried out at different temperatures and the results recorded in the table below.

Temperature / °C	0	10	20	30	40	50	60	70	80
Number of bubbles produced in one minute	0	10	24	40	48	38	8	0	0

(a) Plot a graph of these results on the graph paper. (3)

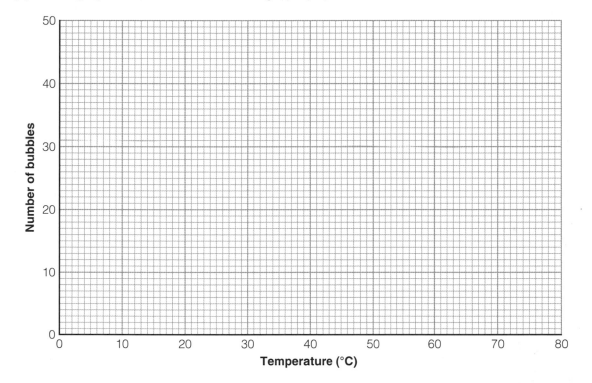

(b) Describe how the number of bubbles produced varies with the temperature of the reacting mixture. (2)

....

....

(c) Using the graph, estimate the optimum temperature for catalase to work at. (1)

....

(d) Factors other than temperature affect the activity of enzymes. Explain why the enzyme amylase, found in saliva, stops working when it gets to the stomach. (2)

....

....

For more help on this topic, see Letts GCSE Biology Revision Guide pages 14–15

Metabolism – enzymes

Module 6

1 Cells rely on diffusion as a way of transporting materials inwards and outwards.

(a) Name **two** substances that move by diffusion **into** animal cells. (2)

.... and ....

(b) Name **one** substance that might diffuse **out** of an animal cell. .... (1)

2 Osmosis is a special case of diffusion involving water. Plants rely on osmosis for movement of materials around their various structures.

On the right is a diagram of three plant cells in the root of a plant. Cell **A** has a higher concentration of water than cell **C**.

(a) Explain how water can keep moving from cell **A** to cell **C**. .... (3)

....

....

(b) Which of the following are examples of osmosis? Tick (✓) the **three** correct options. (3)

Water evaporating from leaves ☐

Water moving from plant cell to plant cell ☐

Mixing pure water and sugar solution ☐

A pear losing water in a concentrated solution of sugar ☐

Water moving from blood plasma to body cells ☐

Sugar being absorbed from the intestine into the blood ☐

3 Rabia is investigating how plant cells respond to being surrounded by different concentrations of sugar solution. She places some rhubarb tissue into pure water and then observes the cells under the microscope.

(a) Describe and explain the appearance of the rhubarb cells. (2)

....

....

(b) Rabia then puts some rhubarb tissue into a strong salt solution. Describe how the cells would change in appearance if she observed them under the microscope. (2)

....

....

For more help on this topic, see Letts GCSE Biology Revision Guide pages 18–19

Cell transport

Module 7

1 This diagram shows a magnified view of the inside of a leaf. Complete the missing labels. (3)

Waxy cuticle

Palisade cells

Stoma

(a) ....

(b) ....

(c) ....

2 Plants all share a basic structure consisting of four main organs.

Describe the function that each organ performs in the plant. (4)

Roots: ....

Stem: ....

Leaf: ....

Flower: ....

3 Describe **three** adaptations of xylem vessels that make them suited to the job they do. (3)

....

....

4 The diagram shows xylem and phloem tissue.

(a) State **one** structural difference between the two tissues. (1)

....

....

Xylem Phloem

Xylem   Phloem

(b) Small, herbivorous insects called aphids are found on plant stems. They have piercing mouthparts that can penetrate down to the phloem.

Explain the reasons for this behaviour. (2)

....

....

Plant tissues, organs and systems

Module 8

For more help on this topic, see Letts GCSE Biology Revision Guide pages 20–21

1 In an experiment, a plant biologist carried out an investigation to measure the rate of transpiration in a privet shoot. She set up three tubes like the one in the diagram, measured their mass and exposed them each to different conditions.

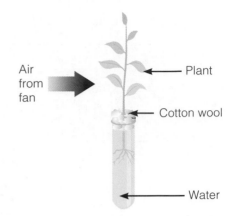

- **A** – Left to stand in a rack

- **B** – Cold moving air from a fan was blown over it

- **C** – A radiant heater was placed next to it

The tubes were left for six hours and then their masses were re-measured. The biologist recorded the masses in this table.

Tube	A	B	C
Mass at start (g)	41	43	45
Mass after six hours (g)	39	35	37
Mass loss (g)	2	8	5
% mass loss	4.9		11.9

(a) Calculate the percentage mass loss in tube B. Show your working. (2)

....

....

(b) Which factor increased the rate of transpiration the most? .... (1)

(c) Evaporation from the leaves has increased in tubes B and C. Describe how this would affect water in the xylem vessels of the plant. (1)

....

2 Guard cells respond to light intensity by opening and closing stomata. Explain how this occurs. In your answer, use ideas about osmosis and turgidity. (6)

....

....

....

....

....

....

Continue your answer for this question on a separate piece of paper.

For more help on this topic, see Letts GCSE Biology Revision Guide pages 22–23

1 The graph shows the number of people who die from coronary heart disease per 100 000 people in different parts of the UK.

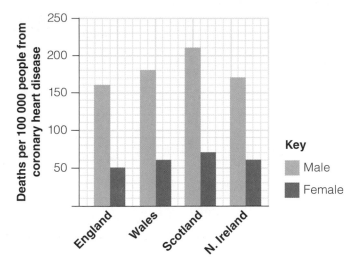

(a) (i) Which country has the highest number of deaths per 100 000? (1)

....

(ii) Calculate the difference between this country's death rate for males and the country with the smallest death rate for males. (1)

....

(b) Describe the pattern between death rates from coronary heart disease in men and women. (1)

....

2 The diagram shows the human circulatory system.

Match the numbers on the diagram with the words listed below. Write the appropriate numbers in the boxes. (4)

Artery ☐

Capillaries in the body ☐

Vein ☐

Capillaries in the lungs ☐

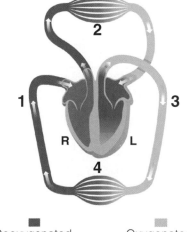

■ Deoxygenated blood   ■ Oxygenated blood

For more help on this topic, see Letts GCSE Biology Revision Guide pages 24–25

1 The table shows some data from an experiment measuring the effect of different doses of warfarin in two samples of rat blood. Warfarin prevents blood from clotting, killing the rat as a result of internal bleeding.

Warfarin dose / mg per kg body weight	Time for clot to form in sample 1	Time for clot to form in sample 2
0.2	52	61
0.4	101	99
0.6	193	197
0.8	300	311
1	978	984

(a) Calculate the average change in clotting rate between 0.2 and 1.0 mg of warfarin per kilogram of body weight. Show your working. (2)

....

....

(b) Explain why the warfarin dose was measured in mg per kg of body weight. (1)

....

(c) Describe the pattern of results shown in the data. (1)

....

2 Scientists are studying the performance of pearl divers living on a Japanese island. They have timed how long they can stay underwater. The scientists have also measured recovery time for the divers' breathing rates after a dive. The data is shown in the table below.

Vital capacity / litres	Max. time under water / mins
3.5	2.5
4.0	2.7
4.3	2.8
4.5	2.9
4.6	3.0

Vital capacity is the maximum volume of air that the lungs can hold at any one time.

One of the scientists suggests that having a larger vital capacity allows a diver to stay underwater for longer. Do you agree with her? Give a reason for your answer. (2)

Agree / disagree: ....

Reason: ....

....

For more help on this topic, see Letts GCSE Biology Revision Guide pages 26–27

HT **1** A student decided that he would test a green plant to see how the rate of photosynthesis changed with temperature. The graph shows the results he obtained.

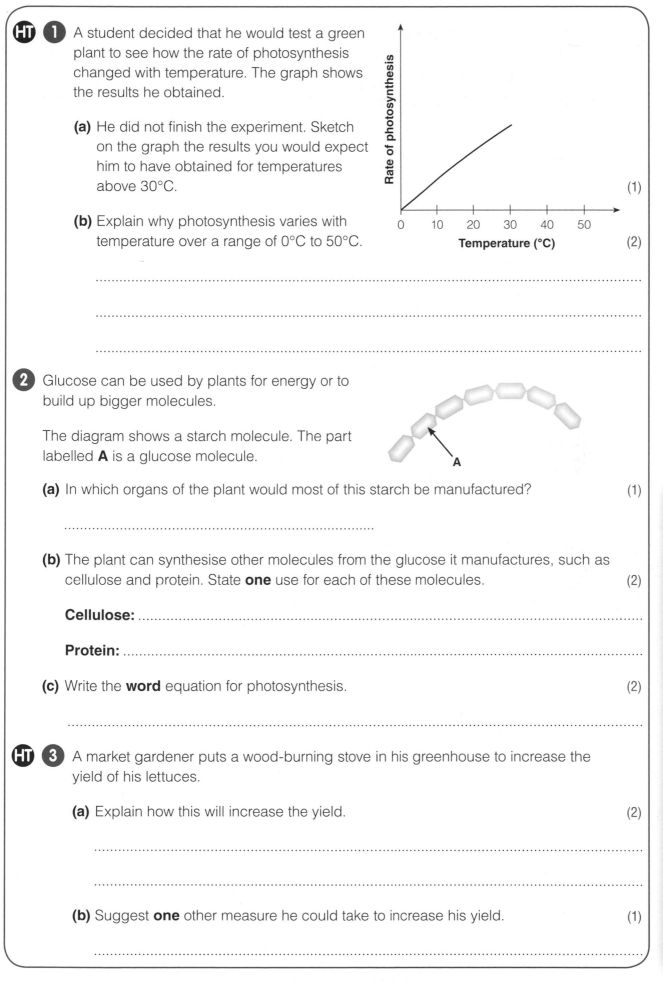

(a) He did not finish the experiment. Sketch on the graph the results you would expect him to have obtained for temperatures above 30°C. (1)

(b) Explain why photosynthesis varies with temperature over a range of 0°C to 50°C. (2)

....

....

....

2 Glucose can be used by plants for energy or to build up bigger molecules.

The diagram shows a starch molecule. The part labelled **A** is a glucose molecule.

(a) In which organs of the plant would most of this starch be manufactured? (1)

....

(b) The plant can synthesise other molecules from the glucose it manufactures, such as cellulose and protein. State **one** use for each of these molecules. (2)

Cellulose: ....

Protein: ....

(c) Write the **word** equation for photosynthesis. (2)

....

HT **3** A market gardener puts a wood-burning stove in his greenhouse to increase the yield of his lettuces.

(a) Explain how this will increase the yield. (2)

....

....

(b) Suggest **one** other measure he could take to increase his yield. (1)

....

For more help on this topic, see Letts GCSE Biology Revision Guide pages 28–29

Photosynthesis

Module 12

1 Obesity is a non-communicable condition. The table shows how obesity in a population of children aged between two and ten changed between 2005–2013.

Year	% of obese children
2005	9.9
2006	10.2
2007	10.8
2008	11.3
2009	11.8
2010	12.3
2011	12.8
2012	13.3
2013	13.7

(a) Predict the percentage of obese children in the UK for 2014 based on this trend. (1)

...........................%

(b) If the body's daily energy requirements are exceeded, sugar can be converted to storage products; for example, fat under the skin.
Name **one** other storage product and where it would be found. (2)

....

(c) Write down **two** other conditions / diseases that are non-communicable. (2)

....

....

2 The table shows how smoking can affect a person's chances of getting lung cancer.

Number of cigarettes smoked per day	Increased chance of lung cancer compared to non-smokers
5	×4
10	×8
15	×12
20	×16

(a) Estimate the increased chance of lung cancer if someone smoked 25 cigarettes a day. (1)

....

(b) Write down **one** harmful effect that smoking can have on unborn babies. (1)

....

....

For more help on this topic, see Letts GCSE Biology Revision Guide pages 32–33

1 Microorganisms consist of bacteria, viruses, fungi and protists. Many cause harm to the human body.

(a) Write down the term that describes these disease-causing organisms. (1)

....

(b) Harmful microorganisms produce symptoms when they reproduce in large numbers. Write down **two** ways in which microorganisms cause these symptoms. (2)

1. ....

2. ....

2 The picture below shows the bacterium that causes cholera.

(a) Write down **two** symptoms of cholera. (2)

1. ....

2. ....

(b) Explain why cholera spreads rapidly in natural disaster zones. (2)

1. ....

2. ....

3 Malaria kills many thousands of people every year. The disease is common in areas that have warm temperatures and stagnant water.

(a) Explain why this is. (2)

....

....

(b) A protist called *Plasmodium* lives in the salivary glands of the female *Anopheles* mosquito.

From the box below, choose a word that describes each organism. (2)

parasite	disease	symptom	vector	consumer	host

Mosquito: .... **Plasmodium:** ....

(c) Samit, an African villager, believes that having mosquito nets around the beds of family members and taking antiviral remedies will reduce their risk of catching malaria.

Explain why he is only partially correct. (2)

....

....

For more help on this topic, see Letts GCSE Biology Revision Guide pages 34–35

1 The diagram shows a white blood cell producing small proteins as part of the body's immune system.

(a) What is the name of these proteins?

.... (1)

(b) These proteins will eventually lock on to specific invading pathogens. Describe what happens next to disable the pathogens. (1)

....

....

(c) Below are the names of some defence mechanisms that the body uses. Match each defence mechanism with the correct function. The first one has been done for you. (3)

Epithelial cells in respiratory passages	engulf pathogens.
Phagocytes	contain enzymes called lysozymes that break down pathogen cells.
Tears	contains acid to break down pathogen cells.
Stomach	trap pathogens in mucus.

2 The graph shows the antibody levels in Dominic after he contracted the flu. The flu pathogen first entered his body two days before point X. There was then a second invasion at point Y.

(a) Name **one** transmission method by which Dominic could have caught the flu virus. (1)

....

(b) After how many days did the antibodies reach their maximum level? (1)

.... days

(c) What is the difference in antibody level between point Y and this maximum? Show your working. (2)

.... arbitrary units

(d) Explain, using your knowledge of memory cells, the difference between these two levels. (2)

....

....

For more help on this topic, see Letts GCSE Biology Revision Guide pages 36–37

Human defences

Module 15

1 The photograph shows the structure of the human immunodeficiency virus (HIV). For decades it has spread throughout the world, especially in developing countries.

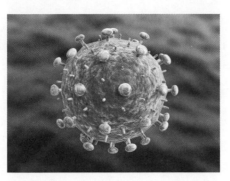

A vaccine is now being developed that shows promising results. It works by mimicing the shapes and structures of HIV proteins. Scientists hope the immune system may be 'educated' to attack the real virus. A specially designed adenovirus shell can protect the vaccine genes until they are in a cell that can produce the vaccine protein.

Using your knowledge of the immune response and immunological memory, describe and explain how antibodies can be produced against the HIV virus. (6)

....

....

....

....

....

....

....

....

....

....

2 Explain why antibiotics are becoming increasingly less effective against 'superbugs' such as MRSA. (3)

....

....

....

....

For more help on this topic, see Letts GCSE Biology Revision Guide pages 38–39

1 A pharmaceutical company is carrying out a clinical trial on a new drug called alketronol. They are testing it to see whether it produces significant adverse (harmful) events in a sample of 226 patients.

(a) Apart from checking for adverse events, write down **two** other reasons that a company carries out clinical trials. (2)

1. ....

2. ....

(b) The kind of trial carried out is a double blind trial. What does this term mean? (2)

....

....

....

(c) Data from the trial is shown in the table below.

Adverse event	Alketronol	Placebo
	Number of patients	Number of patients
Pain	4	3
Cardiovascular	21	20
Dyspepsia	7	6
Rash	10	1

(i) Calculate the percentage of patients **in the trial** who suffered a cardiovascular event while taking alketronol. Show your working. (2)

.... %

(ii) A scientist is worried that alketronol may trigger heart attacks. Is there evidence in the data to support this view? Explain your answer. (2)

....

....

....

(iii) Which other adverse event might cause concern? Give a reason for your decision. (2)

....

....

For more help on this topic, see Letts GCSE Biology Revision Guide pages 40–41

1 Ash dieback, or *Chalara*, is caused by a fungus called *Hymenoscyphus fraxineus*. *Chalara* results in loss of leaves, crown dieback and bark damage in ash trees. Once a tree is infected, the disease is usually fatal because the tree is weakened and becomes prone to pests or pathogens.

The map gives an indication of where cases of *Chalara* were reported in 2012 in the UK.

Scientists have also discovered that:

- *Chalara* spores are unlikely to survive for more than a few days
- spores can be dispersed by winds blowing from mainland Europe
- trees need a high dose of spores to become infected
- there is a low probability of dispersal on clothing or animals and birds.

Key:
■ = infection confirmed

(a) Damage to leaves can be caused by lack of certain minerals that plants need.

Write down **one** mineral deficiency and how it can affect leaves.

Mineral deficiency: ....   **Leaf appearance:** .... (2)

(b) Which **one** of the following conclusions is supported by evidence from the map? Tick (✓) **one** box. (1)

Chalara is limited to the East of England. ☐

Spores of *Chalara* arrived in England by being carried on winds from Europe. ☐

There is a high concentration of *Chalara* cases in the East of England. ☐

Ash trees in north-west Scotland are resistant to *Chalara*. ☐

(c) One scientist suggests that cutting down and burning infected trees could eradicate the disease.

(i) Explain how this method could be effective. (2)

....

....

(ii) Give **one** reason why this control method may not stop the spread of *Chalara*. (1)

....

For more help on this topic, see Letts GCSE Biology Revision Guide pages 42–43

1 From the box below, choose three words to complete the information about how conditions are kept stable in the human body. (3)

effectors	spine	receptors	homeostasis	hormones	glands

Certain factors have to be kept constant in the body. This is achieved by a process called .... In order for this to happen, the central nervous system (CNS) needs to receive information from the environment. This is accomplished through .... such as light-sensitive cells on the retina. Once the information has been relayed, the CNS brings about appropriate changes through ....

HT **2** This diagram shows how production of the hormone adrenaline is controlled.

Hypothalamus → **CRH** Corticotropin-releasing hormone → Pituitary → **ACTH** Adrenocorticotropic hormone → Adrenal glands → **Adrenaline**

(a) What name is given to this process, where a system resists a change from a norm (set point) level? .... (1)

(b) Another hormone, cortisol, is produced by the adrenal glands. Its production is also governed by CRH and ACTH production, in the same way as adrenaline. Cortisol increases nutrient distribution, reduces inflammation, and also takes part in water control. In Addison's disease, the adrenal glands fail to produce enough cortisol.

   (i) What is the effect of Addison's disease on the production of ACTH? (1)

   ....

   (ii) Using the information above, give **one** symptom of Addison's disease. (1)

   ....

   (iii) Here is some data taken from adult blood samples.

Patient	A	B	C	D	E
Cortisol in blood / µg per litre	31.0	19.2	20.5	1.2	16.0

   Which patient is most likely to have Addison's disease? .... (1)

   (iv) A doctor injects some cortisol into this patient's blood, then takes another sample. The reading is now 7 µg per litre. If we assume that the patient has 5 litres of blood in their body, calculate the amount of cortisol in this person's blood. Show your working. (2)

   ....

For more help on this topic, see Letts GCSE Biology Revision Guide pages 46–47

1 Complete the missing labels in this diagram of a motor neurone. (2)

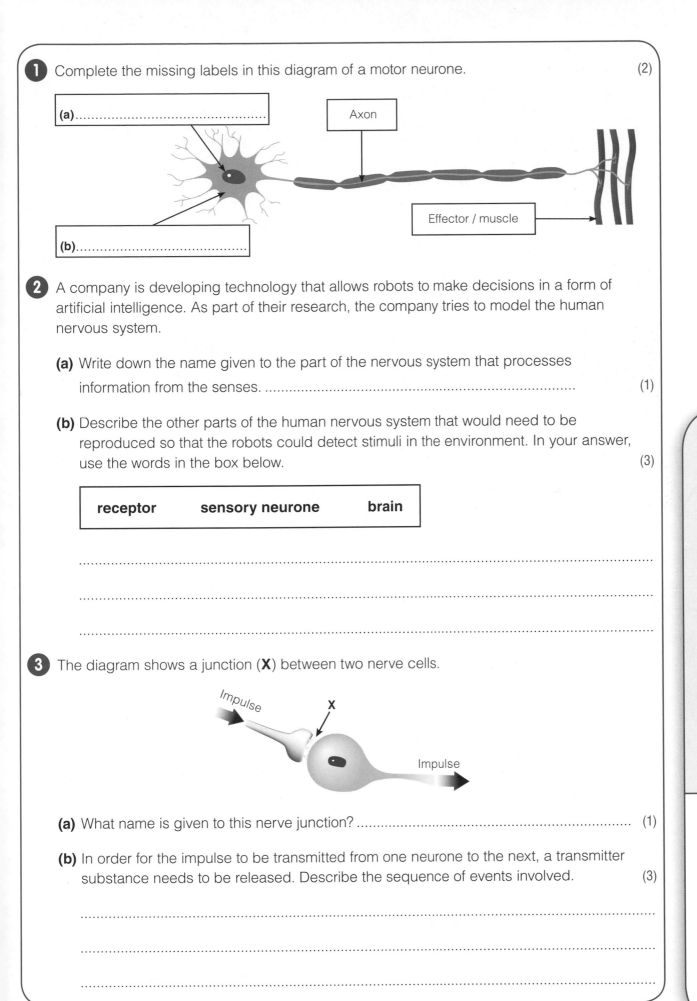

(a)..

Axon

(b)..

Effector / muscle

2 A company is developing technology that allows robots to make decisions in a form of artificial intelligence. As part of their research, the company tries to model the human nervous system.

(a) Write down the name given to the part of the nervous system that processes

information from the senses. .... (1)

(b) Describe the other parts of the human nervous system that would need to be reproduced so that the robots could detect stimuli in the environment. In your answer, use the words in the box below. (3)

receptor	sensory neurone	brain

....

....

....

3 The diagram shows a junction (**X**) between two nerve cells.

Impulse

X

Impulse

(a) What name is given to this nerve junction? .... (1)

(b) In order for the impulse to be transmitted from one neurone to the next, a transmitter substance needs to be released. Describe the sequence of events involved. (3)

....

....

....

For more help on this topic, see Letts GCSE Biology Revision Guide pages 48–49

The nervous system

Module 20

1 The diagram shows the human brain.

(a) Write down the name of the part of the brain labelled X.

.... (1)

X

(b) Tick (✓) the **two** correct statements about the brain and its parts. (2)

The cerebellum is responsible for controlling heartbeat. ☐

The brain contains junctions between all three types of neurone. ☐

The brain is part of the central nervous system. ☐

The medulla controls higher mental functions. ☐

2 Rafiq is enjoying a skiing holiday, but not the cold! His body is working hard to keep at a constant temperature.

(a) After standing while waiting for a ski lift, Rafiq starts to shiver. Explain how shivering helps him to maintain his temperature. (2)

....

....

(b) After skiing cross-country for a while, Rafiq starts to sweat underneath his thermals. Explain how sweating enables him to lose heat. (2)

....

....

(c) Rafiq's internal body temperature has changed very little during the day. What temperature is this likely to be? Circle the correct answer. (1)

| 30°C | 35°C | 37°C | 40°C | 50°C |

(d) Rafiq's blood vessels can undergo vasoconstriction. Explain how this helps him conserve heat. (3)

....

....

....

For more help on this topic, see Letts GCSE Biology Revision Guide pages 50–51

Nervous control

Module 21

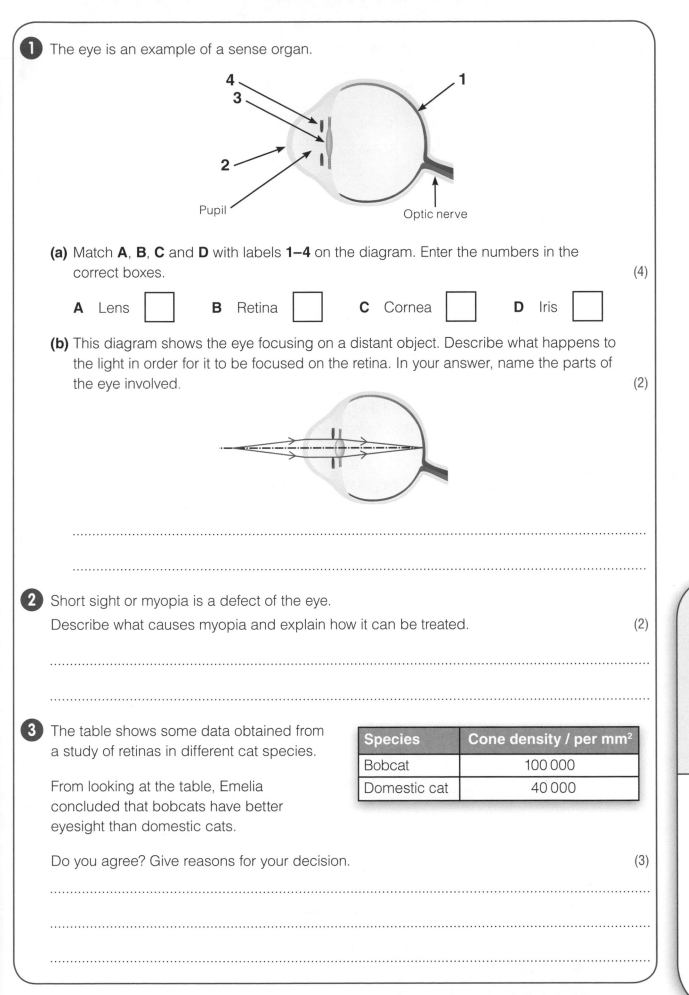

1 The eye is an example of a sense organ.

(a) Match **A**, **B**, **C** and **D** with labels **1–4** on the diagram. Enter the numbers in the correct boxes. (4)

A Lens ☐ **B** Retina ☐ **C** Cornea ☐ **D** Iris ☐

(b) This diagram shows the eye focusing on a distant object. Describe what happens to the light in order for it to be focused on the retina. In your answer, name the parts of the eye involved. (2)

....

....

2 Short sight or myopia is a defect of the eye.

Describe what causes myopia and explain how it can be treated. (2)

....

....

3 The table shows some data obtained from a study of retinas in different cat species.

From looking at the table, Emelia concluded that bobcats have better eyesight than domestic cats.

Do you agree? Give reasons for your decision. (3)

Species	Cone density / per mm²
Bobcat	100 000
Domestic cat	40 000

....

....

....

For more help on this topic, see Letts GCSE Biology Revision Guide pages 52–53

1 Label the gland shown on the diagram and add the name of a hormone it produces. (2)

| Gland: |
| Hormone: |

2 A new nanotechnology device has been developed for people with diabetes – it can detect levels of glucose in the blood and communicate this information to a hormone implant elsewhere in the body. The implant releases a precise quantity of hormone into the bloodstream when required.

(a) Explain how this device could help a person with type 1 diabetes who has just eaten a meal. (2)

....

....

(b) Explain why a person with type 2 diabetes might not have as much use for this technology. (2)

....

....

3 Complete the missing information in the table, which is about different endocrine glands in the body. (4)

Gland	Hormones produced
Pituitary gland	.... and ....
Pancreas	Insulin and glucagon
....	Thyroxine
....	Adrenaline
Ovary	.... and ....
Testes	Testosterone

For more help on this topic, see Letts GCSE Biology Revision Guide pages 54–55

1 A marathon runner is resting the day before she competes in a race. The table shows the water that she gains and loses during the day.

Gained	Water gained (ml)	Lost	Water lost (ml)
In food	1000	In urine	
From respiration	300	In sweat	800
Drinking	1200	In faeces	100
Total gained		**Total lost**	2500

(a) How much water does the runner lose in urine during the day? .... (1)

(b) What can you say about the total water gained and the total water lost in the day? Why is this important? (2)

....

....

(c) The runner runs a marathon the next day. Suggest and explain how the figures shown in the table may alter during the day of the race. (4)

....

....

....

2 The diagram shows a nephron.

Your responses to the following questions should be **A**, **B** or **C**.

(a) Where does selective reabsorption occur? (1)

....

(b) Where does salt regulation occur? .... (1)

(c) In which region does filtration occur? .... (1)

(d) Explain how the brain and kidneys work together to restore water levels in the blood when the body is dehydrated. (4)

....

....

....

For more help on this topic, see Letts GCSE Biology Revision Guide pages 56–57

1. The graph shows the thickness of the uterus during the menstrual cycle. Use the graph and your scientific knowledge to explain what happens in the woman's ovaries and uterus between days 5 and 28. (3)

Uterus wall rich in blood vessels

Thickness of wall

0   5   14   28   5

Day of cycle

....

....

....

2. Match each hormone with the correct description. The first one has been done for you. (3)

FSH	Oestrogen	Progesterone	LH
promotes repair of the uterus wall **and** stimulates egg release.	maintains the lining of the uterus.	stimulates release of an egg **only**.	causes the egg to mature.

HT 3. The diagram shows how the human process of ovulation is controlled.

X   X

Pituitary

Hormone **Y** LH

Ovary

Maturing follicle   Corpus luteum

Oestrogen   *Hormone **Z***

Ovulation

(a) X represents an effect that two hormones have on the pituitary gland. Write down the name of this effect. .... (1)

(b) Name hormone Y. .... (1)

(c) Name hormone Z. .... (1)

(d) Describe the effect on hormone Z if the egg is fertilised. (2)

....

....

For more help on this topic, see Letts GCSE Biology Revision Guide pages 58–59

1 Tim and Margaret are finding it hard to conceive a child. They visit a fertility clinic and meet some other couples. The table shows some information about the problem that each couple has.

Couple	Problem causing infertility	Percentage of infertile couples with this problem	Percentage success rate of treatment
Tim and Margaret	Blocked fallopian tubes	13	20
Rohit and Saleema	Irregular ovulation	16	75
Leroy and Jane	No ovulation	7	95
Gary and Charlotte	Low sperm production	15	10
Ian and Kaye	No sperm production	21	10
Stuart and Mai	Unknown cause	28	–

(a) Which couple has the best chance of being successfully treated? (1)

....

(b) In how many of the six couples is the problem known to be with the female? (1)

....

(c) The treatment of irregular ovulation and no ovulation have the highest success rates. Explain why treating irregular ovulation would produce more pregnancies in the whole population. (2)

....

(d) Leroy and Jane are considering two methods to help them have children. The first is to have an egg donated by another woman. The second is to arrange for another woman to conceive the child using sperm from Leroy, then give birth to it (surrogacy). What are the advantages and disadvantages of each method? (4)

....

....

....

....

....

2 Explain how the contraceptive pill works. In your answer, name any hormones involved. (2)

....

....

....

For more help on this topic, see Letts GCSE Biology Revision Guide pages 60–61

1 Raj germinated a bean seed. Diagram **A** shows the bean after seven days. Raj then turned the bean onto its side (diagram **B**). Diagram **C** shows the bean a week later.

A

B

C

Explain fully why the plant responded in this way. (3)

....

....

....

2 Which substance does rooting powder contain that stimulates root growth?
Tick (✓) **one** box. (1)

Enzymes ☐   Nitrates ☐   Plant hormones ☐   Vitamins ☐

3 Miriam wants to find out if shoots will grow towards the light. Describe an experiment she could do to show this. Your answer should include:

- a method
- the likely results she would get. (6)

....

....

....

....

....

....

....

....

....

For more help on this topic, see Letts GCSE Biology Revision Guide pages 62–63

1 From the box below, choose **three** words to complete these sentences. (3)

| zygotes | gametes | diploid | haploid | mitosis | meiosis |

Eggs and sperm are .... They are .... because they contain one set of chromosomes. Eggs and sperm are produced in the ovaries and testes by ....

2 Tick (✓) the **two** statements about causes of variation that are true. (2)

Meiosis shuffles genes, which makes each gamete unique. ☐

Gametes fuse randomly. ☐

Zygotes fuse randomly. ☐

Mitosis shuffles genes, which makes each gamete the same. ☐

3

Sexual reproduction is the best strategy for organisms because it allows variation and therefore greater adaptation.

Asexual reproduction is better because when an organism is well adapted, it can produce exact copies of itself.

(a) John and Ayesha disagree about which type of reproduction is most beneficial to organisms. State which explanation, if any, is correct. Give the reasons for your choice. (3)

....

....

....

....

(b) Apart from variation, write down **one** other difference between sexual and asexual reproduction. (1)

....

....

(c) Describe how yeast carries out asexual reproduction. (2)

....

....

For more help on this topic, see Letts GCSE Biology Revision Guide pages 66–67

1 Tick (✓) the statements about the Human Genome Project (HGP) that are true. (3)

The genome of an organism is the entire genetic material present in its adult body cells. ☐

The data produced from the HGP produced a listing of amino acid sequences. ☐

The HGP involved collaboration between US and UK geneticists. ☐

The project allowed genetic abnormalities to be tracked between generations. ☐

The project was controversial as it relied on embryonic stem cells. ☐

2 Studies of genomes can help scientists work out the evolutionary history of organisms by comparing the similarity of particular DNA sequences that code for a specific protein.

The table shows the percentage DNA coding similarity for protein A in different organisms.

Species	% DNA coding similarity between species and humans for protein A
Human	100
Chimpanzee	100
Horse	88.5
Fish	78.6
Yeast	67.3
Protist	56.6

(a) What evidence is there in the table that closely related organisms developed from a recent common ancestor? (1)

....

(b) Using only the information from the table, which non-vertebrate is the most closely related to humans? .... (1)

3 The Human Genome Project has enabled specific genes to be identified that increase the risk of developing cancer in later life. Two of these genes are the *BRCA1* and *BRCA2* mutations that increase the risk of developing breast cancer.

(a) If women are prepared to take a genetic test, how could this information help doctors advise women about breast cancer? (2)

....

....

(b) If a woman possesses these mutations, it does not mean that she will definitely develop breast cancer. Why is this? (2)

....

....

For more help on this topic, see Letts GCSE Biology Revision Guide pages 68–69

1 The molecule DNA is a double helix made of two complementary strands.

(a) Write down the bases that pair with **T** and **C**. (1)

T pairs with ....

C pairs with ....

(b) How many bases code for **one** amino acid when a protein molecule is made? .... (1)

HT **2** Mutations occur when genes on DNA cause them to code for different proteins (or sequences of amino acids).

(a) State **two** causes of mutation. (2)

.... and ....

(b) A change occurs in a section of DNA that leads to a new protein being formed. Explain how this is possible and why the protein is not able to perform its function. (3)

....

....

....

HT **3** The diagram shows the processes that occur in the cell when a protein is coded for and produced. For each of the stages (1–4), describe and explain how the various molecules are involved. (4)

Stage 1: ....

....

Stage 2: ....

....

Stage 3: ....

....

Stage 4: ....

....

For more help on this topic, see Letts GCSE Biology Revision Guide pages 70–71

The genetic code

Module 30

1 Raj is the owner of two dogs, both of which are about two years old. Both dogs are black in colour and came from the same litter of puppies.

(a) A dog's adult body cell contains 78 chromosomes. How many chromosomes would be in a male dog's sperm cells? (1)

....

(b) The dogs' mother had white fur and the father had black fur. Using what you know about dominant genes, suggest why there were no white puppies in the litter. (2)

....

....

HT (c) One year later, one of the black puppies mated with a white-haired dog. She had four puppies. Two had black fur and two had white fur. The letters **B** and **b** represent the alleles for fur colour: **B** for black fur and **b** for white fur.

Draw a fully labelled genetic diagram to explain this. Show which offspring would be black and which would be white. (3)

2 Complete these two different crosses between a brown-eyed parent and a blue-eyed parent. (4)

(a) Brown eyes × Blue eyes

Parents (BB) × (bb)

Gametes

Offspring

Phenotype

(b) Brown eyes × Blue eyes

Parents (Bb) × (bb)

Gametes

Offspring

Phenotype

For more help on this topic, see Letts GCSE Biology Revision Guide pages 72–73

1 This is an evolutionary tree for some of our present-day vertebrates. Where possible, use the diagram to answer these questions.

Million years ago		Geological time period
	Turtle Terrapin Tortoise Snake Lizard Birds Crocodile	
50		Tertiary
	Tuarta (giant lizard)	
		Cretaceous
100		
	Crocodilia	
	Dinosaurs	Jurassic
150		
		Triassic
200	Testudina	Permian
	Archosaurs	
250		
		Carboniferous
300	Sauropods	

(a) How many millions of years ago did the testudina appear? (1)

....

(b) (i) In what geological time period did the dinosaurs become extinct? (1)

....

(ii) How do scientists know that dinosaurs once lived on Earth? (1)

....

(c) What group of animals alive today is most closely related to the snake? (1)

....

(d) Which ancestor is shared by dinosaurs, crocodiles and the giant lizard, but is not an ancestor of tortoises? (1)

....

For more help on this topic, see Letts GCSE Biology Revision Guide pages 74–75

1 Peppered moths are usually pale and speckled. They are often found amongst the lichens on silver birch tree bark. The data below estimates the average number of peppered moths spotted in a city centre before and after the Industrial Revolution.

Month	Before Industrial Revolution		After Industrial Revolution	
	Pale	Dark	Pale	Dark
June	1261	102	87	1035
July	1247	126	108	1336
August	1272	93	72	1019

(a) Complete the table by calculating the mean number of each colour of moth during the summer months. (2)

Before Industrial Revolution		After Industrial Revolution	
Pale	Dark	Pale	Dark
....	....	....	....

(b) Draw a bar graph to represent your results. (2)

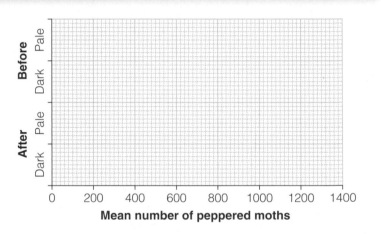

(c) Why do you think there were more pale-coloured moths than dark-coloured moths before the Industrial Revolution? (1)

....

(d) Explain why the number of dark-coloured peppered moths increased significantly during the Industrial Revolution. (2)

....

....

....

2 Lucy is an early hominid fossil that is 3.2 million years old. Why was this a significant find? (1)

....

For more help on this topic, see Letts GCSE Biology Revision Guide pages 76–77

1 From the box below, choose the correct words to complete these sentences. (2)

| selection | adapted | slow | genes | evolved |

Evolution suggests that all living things have .... from simple life forms developed billions of years ago. The process is .... and continual. Organisms that are better .... to their environment are more likely to survive. Adaptations are coded for by .... and can therefore be passed on to offspring.

2 Neo-Darwinists are scientists who have accepted Darwin's theory of natural selection but have built upon it with new ideas. They have developed the theory because of new evidence that has been found.

One of Darwin's main ideas was that successful characteristics can be passed on to the next generation. How might studies of inheritance have provided further evidence for this? (1)

....

....

3 **(a)** Cloning can occur naturally. Which type of cell division is involved in natural cloning? (1)

....

(b) Suggest why asexual reproduction could be useful to commercial plant growers. (2)

....

....

(c) Describe **two** disadvantages of commercial cloning. (2)

....

....

....

....

4 It is illegal to clone human embryos beyond 14 days old.
Suggest **one** reason why this is the case. (1)

....

....

Evolution

Module 34

For more help on this topic, see Letts GCSE Biology Revision Guide pages 78–79

1 (a) A sheep farmer wants to breed sheep that grow high quality wool. What four stages of selective breeding can he use to produce his desired variety? (3)

The first stage has been done for you.

1. Choose males and females that produce good quality wool.

2. ....

3. ....

4. ....

(b) Apart from high quality wool, name another characteristic that a farmer might want to selectively breed into his flock. (1)

....

2 Describe how genetic engineering is different from selective breeding. (2)

....

....

....

3 Explain the benefit of each of these examples of genetic engineering.

(a) Resistance to herbicide in soya plants (1)

....

....

(b) Inserting beta-carotene genes into rice plants (1)

....

....

4 Some people think that genetically engineering resistance to herbicides in plants could have unforeseen consequences. Give **one** example of a harmful effect. (1)

....

....

....

For more help on this topic, see Letts GCSE Biology Revision Guide pages 80–81

1 Lions, tigers and leopards are all carnivorous big cats. They have five toes on their front paws and four toes on their back paws. Their claws can be drawn back to avoid damage. They all roar. Tigers and leopards tend to be solitary animals but lions live in prides of females with one dominant male.

(a) Underline **one** piece of evidence from the information above that suggests that lions, tigers and leopards are all descended from a common ancestor. (1)

(b) This table shows how some scientists have named four species of large cat.

	Genus	Species
Lion	Panthera	leo
Tiger	Panthera	tigris
Leopard	Panthera	pardus
Snow leopard	Uncia	uncia

Are leopards more closely related to tigers or snow leopards? Explain your answer. (2)

....

....

....

2 Archaeopteryx is an ancient fossilised species of bird. When first discovered, scientists found it hard to classify.

Using features shown in the picture, explain why Archaeopteryx is difficult to classify. (2)

....

....

....

For more help on this topic, see Letts GCSE Biology Revision Guide pages 82–83

Classification

Module 36

1 Complete the following passage about adaptations using words from the box below. (3)

| environment | population | features | community | characteristics |
| survival | evolutionary | predatory | suited |

Adaptations are special .... or .... that make a living organism particularly well .... to its .... Adaptations are part of an .... process that increases a living organism's chance of ....

2 A new species of insectivorous mammal has been discovered in Borneo. It has been observed in rainforest undergrowth and more open savannah-like areas. Scientists have called the creature a *long-nosed batink*. They have studied its diet and obtained this data.

Food	Ants	Termites	Aphids	Beetles	Maggots	Bugs	Grubs
Mass eaten per day / g	275	380	320	75	150	20	110

(a) Plot the data for termites, beetles, bugs and grubs as a bar chart. (3)

(b) Calculate the percentage of the batink's diet that is made up from termites. Show your working. (2)

.... %

(c) From what you know about the batink, suggest **two** behavioural adaptations it might have that makes it successful. (2)

....

....

For more help on this topic, see Letts GCSE Biology Revision Guide pages 86–87

1 A meadow supports a wide variety of animals and plants. George is carrying out a survey of the meadow to assess the populations of organisms found there.

(a) State the term that describes the meadow as a place for organisms to live. (1)

....

(b) Which word describes the different populations in the meadow and their interaction with the physical factors found there? (1)

....

(c) George has laid pitfall traps in the meadow to capture and count soil invertebrates. He notices that there are many flying insects that are too difficult to count and identify.

Suggest an item of apparatus he could use to survey the flying insects. (1)

....

(d) George uses a 0.25 m² quadrat to survey the plant populations. He lays ten quadrats in one corner of the field and finds a mean count of 16 meadow buttercups per quadrat. He estimates the area of the meadow to be 5000 m².

Calculate the expected number of buttercups in the whole meadow.
Show your working. (2)

....

....

(e) George finds these two invertebrates in his pitfall traps.

Beetle   Snail

(i) The beetle feeds off other insects. Explain how a decrease in the number of beetles will eventually result in their numbers rising. (2)

....

....

(ii) Thrushes eat snails and worms. Describe what would happen to the number of snails if large numbers of thrushes arrived in their habitat. (1)

....

For more help on this topic, see Letts GCSE Biology Revision Guide pages 88–91

1 The diagram shows a digester that can make use of human sewage. The gas produced from this vessel contains a mixture of 60% methane and 40% carbon dioxide.

(a) What is the name of this type of biofuel? (1)

....

(b) Give **two** uses of this biofuel. (2)

1. ....

2. ....

(c) Explain why these types of digesters are useful in remote parts of the world. (1)

....

2 A group of students wanted to investigate factors affecting decay. They mixed soil with small discs cut from leaves. They divided the leaf disc / soil mixture equally into four test tubes, as shown below.

(a) In which tube would you expect the leaf discs to decay fastest? Give a reason for your answer. .... (2)

....

(b) The students did not add any microorganisms to the test tubes. Where will the microorganisms that cause decay come from? (1)

....

(c) Why did the students seal the tubes with muslin cloth instead of a rubber bung? (1)

....

(d) Suggest **one** way in which the students could use the leaf discs to measure the rate of decay. (1)

....

For more help on this topic, see Letts GCSE Biology Revision Guide pages 92–93

1 Circle the renewable resources. (1)

     water   minerals   oil   wind   coal   wood

2 Explain how rising average global temperatures may have an effect on the Earth. Use the headings below to structure your answer. (3)

Climate zones around the world:

....

....

Sea levels:

....

....

Ice caps and glaciers:

....

....

3 At the moment, the human population is increasing exponentially.

Population / ....

1800   **Time / year**

(a) Sketch a graph that shows this increase. (2)

(b) On the *y*-axis, add a suitable unit for the population. (1)

(c) Suggest **two** reasons for this 'population explosion'. (2)

....

....

For more help on this topic, see Letts GCSE Biology Revision Guide page 94

1 In Ireland, four species of bumble bee are now endangered. Scientists are worried that numbers may become so low that they are inadequate to provide pollination to certain plants.

State **two** reasons why some organisms become endangered. (2)

....

....

2 **(a)** What is deforestation? Tick (✓) the correct definition. (1)

Planting new trees ☐

Forest fires caused by hot weather ☐

Cutting down large areas of forest ☐

Polluting national parks with litter ☐

(b) Which of the following is a consequence of deforestation? Tick (✓) the correct answer. (1)

Decrease in soil erosion in tropical regions ☐

Increase in atmospheric carbon dioxide ☐

Increase in average rainfall ☐

Increase in habitat area ☐

3 Other than using wood for timber, give **two** other reasons for large-scale deforestation. (2)

....

....

4 Circle the correct options in the sentences below. (6)

When deforestation occurs in **tropical / arctic / desert** regions, it has a devastating impact on the environment.

The loss of **trees / animals / insects** means less photosynthesis takes place, so less **oxygen / nitrogen / carbon dioxide** is removed from the atmosphere.

It also leads to a reduction in **variation / biodiversity / mutation**, because some species may become **protected / damaged / extinct** and **habitats / land / farms** are destroyed.

5 Sometimes when land has been cleared of forests to grow crops, farmers stop producing good yields after a few years. Explain why. (1)

....

....

For more help on this topic, see Letts GCSE Biology Revision Guide page 95

1 The picture shows the energy intake and use for a cow.

2000 kJ used by the cow for other purposes

6000 kJ intake

New growth

3000 kJ in faeces

(a) What type of energy does the cow's intake consist of? Tick (✓) the correct answer. (1)

Chemical energy ☐   Potential energy ☐

Light energy ☐   Heat energy ☐

(b) Using the formula below, calculate the energy efficiency for the cow. Show your working. (2)

$$\text{energy efficiency} = \frac{\text{energy used usefully for new growth}}{\text{total energy taken in}} \times 100\%$$

....

....

(c) Humans do not need to eat as much biomass as cows do. Explain why. (2)

....

....

(d) Use your responses to **(b)** and **(c)** to explain why eating cereals and grains is more energy-efficient than eating meat. In your answer, explain the implications for agricultural land use if significant numbers of a population are vegetarian. (6)

....

....

....

....

....

....

....

....

....

For more help on this topic, see Letts GCSE Biology Revision Guide pages 96–97

Energy and biomass in ecosystems

Module 42

1 Some scientists studied the numbers of cod caught in cool to temperate waters in the northern hemisphere. They obtained the following data, which is expressed in a graph.

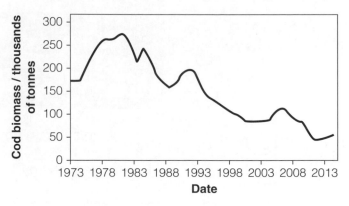

(a) What was the estimated cod biomass in 1988? (1)

.... thousand tonnes

(b) Describe the change in cod numbers between 1988 and 2013. (2)

....

....

(c) International fishing quotas are set in order to manage the numbers of fish in our seas. The table shows data about fishing quotas set by an international fishing commission.

Fish species	UK quota 2013 / tonnes	UK quota 2014 / tonnes
Cod	11 216	13 123
Haddock	27 507	23 381
Whiting	8426	3287

(i) By how much did the cod quota change between 2013 and 2014? (1)

.... tonnes

(ii) Suggest possible reasons for the decreased quota for haddock. (2)

....

....

(d) Suggest **one** other measure that fisheries councils could take to prevent over-fishing. (1)

....

For more help on this topic, see Letts GCSE Biology Revision Guide pages 98–99

GCSE (9–1)
Biology
Paper 1

Higher tier

Time: 1 hour 45 minutes

You may use:

- a calculator
- a ruler.

Instructions

- Use black ink or black ball-point pen. Draw diagrams in pencil.
- Read each question carefully before you start to write your answer.
- Answer **all** questions in the spaces provided.
- Show your working in any calculator question and include units in your answer where appropriate.
- In questions marked with an asterisk (*), marks will be awarded for your ability to structure your answer logically, showing how the points that you make are related or follow on from each other where appropriate.

Information

- The marks for each question are shown in brackets.
  Use this as a guide to how much time to spend on each question.
- The maximum mark for this paper is 100.
- Diagrams are not accurately drawn unless otherwise stated.

Name: _____

1 **(a)** Which substance is a product of anaerobic respiration in humans? Tick (✓) **one** box. **[1]**

Carbon dioxide ☐

Ethanol ☐

Glucose ☐

Lactic acid ☐

(b) Which substance is a product of aerobic respiration in plants? Tick (✓) **one** box. **[1]**

Carbon dioxide ☐

Ethanol ☐

Glucose ☐

Lactic acid ☐

2

Figure 1

(a) Niamh in **Figure 1** is training for a marathon. Every few days she runs a long distance. This builds up the number of mitochondria in her muscle cells.

What is the advantage for Niamh of having extra mitochondria in her muscle cells?
Tick (✓) **one** box. **[1]**

Her muscles become stronger. ☐

Her muscles can contract faster. ☐

Her muscles can release more energy. ☐

Her muscles can repair faster after injury. ☐

*(b) Bob in **Figure 2** has been running hard and has an oxygen debt. Describe what causes an oxygen debt after a session of vigorous exercise and how Bob can recover from its effects.   [3]

Figure 2

....

....

....

....

*(c) Tariq is competing in a 10-mile running race. His heart rate and breathing rate increase. Describe how this helps his muscles during the race.   [3]

....

....

....

3 Which of the following structures are in the correct size order, starting with the smallest?
Tick (✓) **one** box.   [1]

cell, tissue, organ, system ☐

tissue, organ, system, cell ☐

cell, organ, system, tissue ☐

tissue, system, cell, organ ☐

4 Which part of the blood helps protect the body from pathogens?
Tick (✓) **one** box.   [1]

Plasma ☐

Platelets ☐

Red blood cells ☐

White blood cells ☐

5 **(a)** From which section of the human heart is blood pumped to the lungs?
Tick (✓) **one** box. [1]

Left atrium ☐

Right atrium ☐

Left ventricle ☐

Right ventricle ☐

(b) Explain why the left side of the heart is more muscular than the right side. [1]

....

....

(c) The heart contains a number of valves.

Describe how the valves help the heart pump blood more effectively. [1]

....

....

(d) There are around 105 650 deaths in the UK from smoking-related causes each year. The number of deaths due to cardiovascular disease that is linked to smoking is estimated to be 22 100.

What percentage of deaths from smoking each year is due to cardiovascular disease? Show your working. Give your answer to two significant figures. [2]

....

(e) The chance of heart disease can be reduced by lowering alcohol intake and by not smoking. Write about **two** other choices that can be made to reduce the chance of heart disease. [2]

....

....

6 **(a)** Explain how skin defends the human body against disease. [2]

....

....

(b) Disease can be caused by bacteria. Bacteria multiply very quickly – the numbers of cholera bacteria can double every 20 minutes.

Ten cholera bacteria were kept in ideal conditions for growth. How many cholera bacteria were there after two hours? Show your working. **[2]**

....

....

(c) Explain why measles cannot be treated with antibiotics. **[2]**

....

....

(d) Figure 3 shows a photomicrograph of the bacterium *E. coli*, which is a common cause of stomach upsets. The magnification of the photo is × 5000.

Figure 3

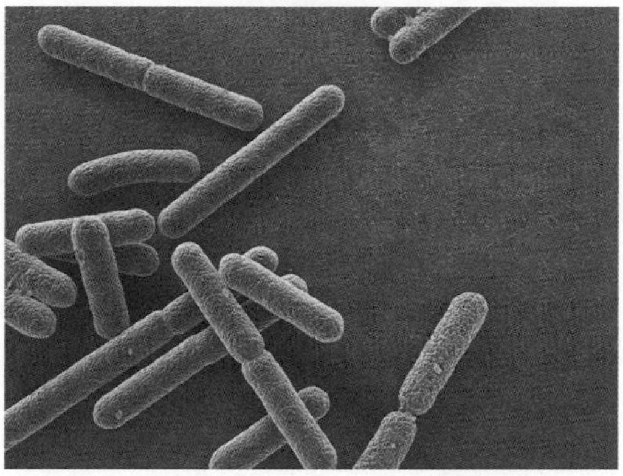

The average magnified length of the bacteria shown in **Figure 3** is 10 mm. Calculate the actual length of an *E. coli* bacterium in μm (1 μm = 1×10^{-3} mm). Show your working. **[2]**

....

....

(e) The spread of cholera is often a problem in temporary refugee camps. One way cholera is spread is through contaminated water.

What simple measures can be taken to reduce the spread of cholera in the camps? **[2]**

....

....

(f) If a disease is infectious, an epidemic can be prevented by vaccination.

Explain why a very high percentage of the population need to be vaccinated for the prevention to be successful. **[2]**

....

....

7 Which of the following is found in a plant cell but not in an animal cell?
Tick (✓) **one** box. [1]

Cell membrane ☐

Cytoplasm ☐

Nucleus ☐

Cell wall ☐

*8 Describe the aseptic method used to grow a colony of bacteria cells from pond water using a sterilised petri dish containing nutrient agar jelly. [4]

....

....

....

....

9 Human stem cell research could lead to new treatments for conditions such as diabetes.

(a) Outline **two** reasons why some people think that human stem cell research should not be allowed. [2]

....

....

(b) Look at **Figure 4**. What is the name of the process by which a stem cell becomes a new cell type? [1]

Figure 4

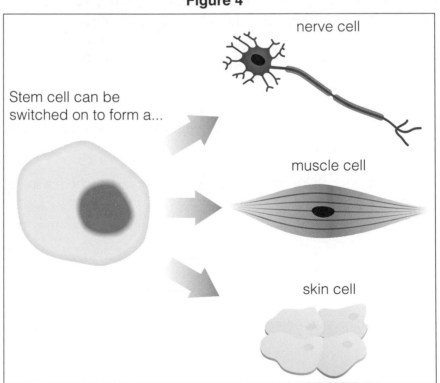

....

10 **(a)** Stomata are found on the underside of a plant leaf. During the day the stomata open to allow carbon dioxide into the leaf. Outline how the stomata open. **[2]**

....

....

(b) Carbon dioxide moves into a leaf by diffusion. Describe the process of diffusion. **[2]**

....

....

11 **(a)** **Figure 5** shows a celery plant. The stalk of a celery plant contains xylem vessels.

Figure 5

Describe the structure of xylem vessels. **[2]**

....

....

(b) Describe how root cells are adapted to allow the efficient absorption of water. **[2]**

....

....

12 **Figure 6** shows an experiment to investigate how water is taken up by a plant.

Figure 6

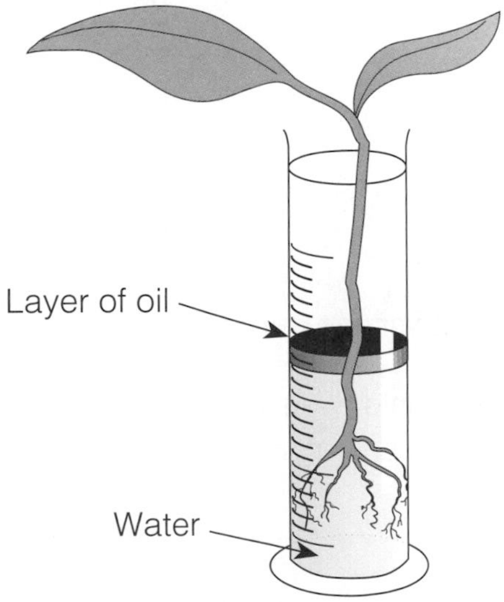

Layer of oil

Water

(a) What is the purpose of the layer of oil? **[1]**

....

(b) Table 1 shows the results of the experiment.

Table 1

Time (days)	0	1	2	3	4
Volume of water in cylinder (cm³)	50	47	43	42	40

Calculate the average water loss per day from the measuring cylinder in **Figure 6**.
Show your working. **[2]**

....

....

Average water loss: .... cm³ per day

13 **Figure 7** shows a sheepdog puppy. There are 39 pairs of chromosomes in the skin cell of a sheepdog puppy. Two of the chromosomes determine the sex of the puppy.

Figure 7

(a) How many chromosomes are there in the sperm cell of a sheepdog? Tick (✓) **one** box. **[1]**

39 ☐

76 ☐

78 ☐

80 ☐

(b) The number of skin cells increases as the puppy grows.

A skin cell grows and then divides into two skin cells. What is the name of this process?
Explain why each skin cell has the same number of chromosomes. **[4]**

....

....

....

....

14 Genetically engineered bacteria can be used to make human insulin to treat diabetes. The human genes to make insulin are inserted into the bacteria DNA.

Outline **three** reasons why bacteria are chosen for this process. **[3]**

....

....

....

15 In a recent newspaper article, the following statement appeared:

You can only get cancer if you have the wrong genes.

This is not true.

Write down **three** other factors that could be involved in the formation of cancer cells. **[3]**

....

....

....

16 **(a)** Which of the following substances breaks down starch during digestion?
Tick (✓) **one** box. **[1]**

Amylase ☐

Cellulose ☐

Lipase ☐

Protease ☐

*(b) Describe the simple chemical steps that convert plant protein in your diet into a human protein such as collagen. **[4]**

....

....

....

....

(c) A new biological washing powder (see **Figure 8**) contains protease and lipase enzymes. It is very good at removing food stains from clothing in a 30 °C wash.

Figure 8

Explain why the washing powder is less effective when used in a 60 °C wash. **[2]**

....

....

17 Plants and animals use glucose for respiration. Plants also convert glucose into different substances. Name **three** of these substances and give a reason why each one is important. **[3]**

....

....

....

18 **Figure 9** shows an experiment to demonstrate osmosis.

Figure 9

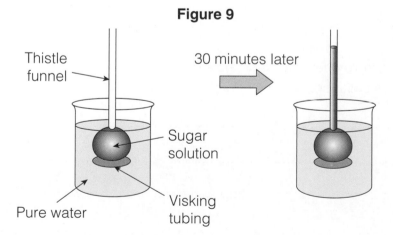

Explain why the volume of solution inside the thistle funnel has increased. **[3]**

....

....

....

*19 Black spot is a fungal disease that affects rose leaves (see **Figure 10**). Fatima has noticed that roses growing in areas with high air pollution are less affected by the disease. She thinks that regular exposure to acid rain is stopping the disease from developing.

Figure 10

Describe a simple experiment that Fatima could carry out to test her theory. [3]

....

....

....

....

20 The foxglove plant contains toxic substances that, if eaten, cause the heart to slow down or even stop. What is the benefit to the plant of being poisonous? [1]

....

21 (a) A farmer has tested the soil in one of his fields and found that it does not have enough nitrate content for his next crop. What will be the effect on his crop if he does nothing about it? [1]

....

(b) The farmer researches what type of manure he could use on his field. He only wants to use manure that comes from his own farm animals. **Table 2** shows his findings.

Table 2

Animal	Cow	Horse	Poultry	Rabbit
Percentage of nitrate in manure	0.7	0.8	2.1	2.0
Number of animals on the farm	120	5	220	35

Outline **one** advantage and **one** disadvantage of using rabbit manure on the field. [2]

....

....

22 **(a)** Thomas burns paraffin in a small stove inside his greenhouse during March and April.
How does this benefit the growth of his greenhouse plants? **[2]**

....

....

(b) Complete the balanced symbol equation for photosynthesis. **[2]**

$$6\,CO_2 + \text{.....................} \longrightarrow C_6H_{12}O_6 + \text{.....................}$$

*(c) Anoushka investigates the effect of light on photosynthesis at 25 °C.
She uses the apparatus shown in **Figure 11**.

Figure 11

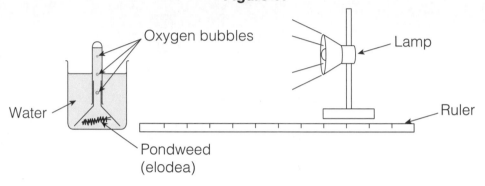

She moves the lamp and counts the bubbles at different distances from the pondweed.
Table 3 shows her results.

Table 3

Distance from lamp to pondweed (cm)	Number of bubbles counted in five minutes
10	241
20	124
30	60
40	36
50	24

Describe the pattern in the results in **Table 3** and predict how the pattern would change if the experiment was repeated at 35 °C and at 55 °C. Explain your answers. **[6]**

....

....

....

....

....

....

....

....

....

....

23 **Figure 12** shows the antigens of a pathogen.

Figure 12

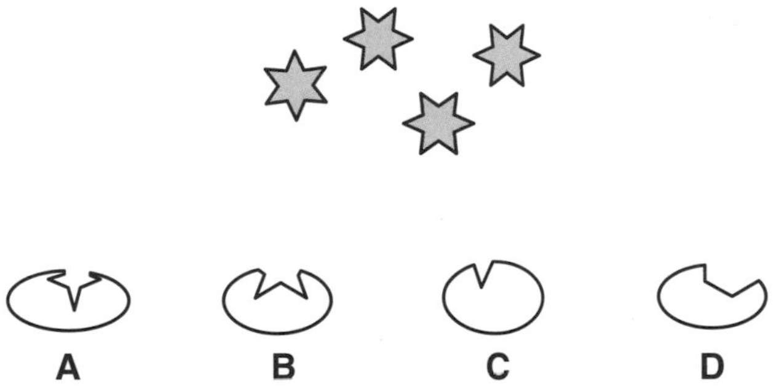

A   **B**   **C**   **D**

(a) Look at images A–D, which show the binding site of four Y-shaped antibodies. Which antibody will the body make to protect itself from the disease caused by the pathogen?
Tick (✓) **one** box. **[1]**

A ☐

B ☐

C ☐

D ☐

(b) A vaccine contains the pathogen that causes the disease. Explain why the patient does not develop the disease when being treated with a vaccine. **[1]**

....

24 Outline why it is difficult to develop drugs that disable or destroy viruses. **[2]**

....

....

25 The development of certain types of breast cancer are aided by the over production in the body of a particular enzyme called HER2.

A drug containing a monoclonal antibody has been developed that reduces the activity of HER2 in the body.

*(a) Explain how the drug reduces the activity of the enzyme in the patient. **[3]**

....

....

....

....

(b) When this drug went to the clinical trial stage of testing, it was tested in a 'double blind' trial.

Describe how a 'double blind' trial is carried out and explain why it is more effective than a simple blind trial. **[3]**

....

....

....

....

TOTAL FOR PAPER = 100 MARKS

GCSE (9–1)
Biology
Paper 2

Higher tier

Time: 1 hour 45 minutes

You may use:

- a calculator
- a ruler.

Instructions

- Use black ink or black ball-point pen. Draw diagrams in pencil.
- Read each question carefully before you start to write your answer.
- Answer **all** questions in the spaces provided.
- Show your working in any calculator question and include units in your answer where appropriate.
- In questions marked with an asterisk (*), marks will be awarded for your ability to structure your answer logically, showing how the points that you make are related or follow on from each other where appropriate.

Information

- The marks for each question are shown in brackets.
  Use this as a guide to how much time to spend on each question.
- The maximum mark for this paper is 100.
- Diagrams are not accurately drawn unless otherwise stated.

Name: ....

1 **Figure 1** shows a simple food chain. The arrows represent the transfer of energy in the food chain.

Figure 1

Sun   A   Grass   B   Rabbit   C   Stoat   D   Fox

Which arrow shows the greatest transfer of energy?
Tick (✓) **one** box. [1]

A ☐

B ☐

C ☐

D ☐

2 **Figure 2** shows a flock of seagulls. The number of seagulls in a flock is affected by both abiotic and biotic factors.

Figure 2

Which of the following is a biotic factor?
Tick (✓) **one** box. [1]

Temperature ☐

Rainfall ☐

Disease ☐

Ocean tides ☐

3 Polar bears live in the Arctic. As **Figure 3** shows, they are often found on ice floes where they hunt seals.

Figure 3

Describe **two** adaptations that help polar bears survive in the arctic wilderness. [2]

....

....

4 An ecologist surveys a meadow to determine the number of field voles living there.

Humane traps are set and after 8 hours, 15 voles have been captured.

Each vole is marked by shaving a small section of fur from its back and is then released.

The traps are set again.

After a further 8 hours, 21 voles are captured. Four of these have shaved backs.

Use this formula to calculate the number of field voles in the meadow:

number in first sample × number in second sample
number in second sample previously marked

Show your working. [2]

....

....

5 (a) Most of the salmon sold in supermarkets comes from fish farms. The salmon are raised in large cages containing thousands of salmon.

Outline **one** advantage and **one** problem of using this method of farming fish. [2]

....

....

(b) Fish farming is seen as a sustainable method of providing fish for the table. Due to overfishing, 'wild' fish stocks are declining quickly.

Describe what measures are now being taken to preserve 'wild' fish stocks. **[2]**

....

....

6 | **Figure 4** shows a kakapo (*Strigops habroptilus*), which is a flightless parrot found only on a few small islands in New Zealand.

Figure 4

(a) Using the Linnaean system, what is the genus of the Kakapo? Tick (✓) **one** box. **[1]**

Animalia ☐

Aves ☐

Strigops ☐

habroptilus ☐

(b) The kakapo is a herbivore. It lives in woodland and is an excellent tree climber.

What part does the kakapo play in the woodland ecosystem? Tick (✓) **one** box. **[1]**

Decomposer ☐

Primary consumer ☐

Producer ☐

Secondary consumer ☐

(c) The kakapo has been threatened with extinction for over one hundred years. It has become an endangered species since Europeans brought animals such as cats, dogs and rats into New Zealand.

Use ideas about genetics to explain why it has not evolved to escape from new predators. **[3]**

....

....

....

7 The following text is one of the instructions on a packet of antibiotic tablets (see **Figure 5**):
Complete the prescribed course of treatment as directed by your doctor.

Figure 5

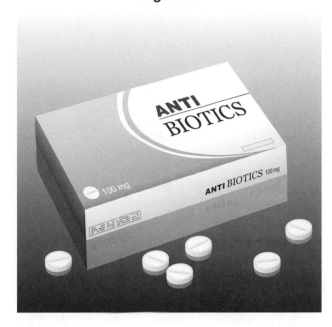

Explain why this instruction is important to stop bacteria becoming resistant to this antibiotic. **[3]**

....

....

....

8 Why are fossils only found in sedimentary rocks? **[1]**

....

....

9 Outline **two** reasons why Darwin's theory of evolution took many years to gain acceptance by the scientific community. **[2]**

....

....

10 What activity is the cerebellum area of the brain associated with?
Tick (✓) **one** box. **[1]**

Control of breathing ☐

Consciousness ☐

Memory ☐

Control of movement ☐

11 **Figure 6** shows some of the endocrine system.

Figure 6

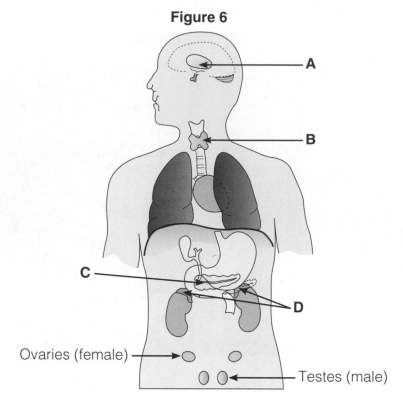

Ovaries (female)

Testes (male)

Which label shows the adrenal gland?
Tick (✓) **one** box. [1]

A ☐

B ☐

C ☐

D ☐

*12 A sauna is a very hot, small, wooden room, typically heated to above 80 °C (see **Figure 7**). Sitting in a sauna is good for relaxing muscles and helps to cleanse the skin.

Figure 7

In Finland people sit in a sauna for up to 20 minutes and then go outside and plunge into icy cold water.

Describe how the body responds to heating up in the sauna and the changes that happen as it cools rapidly in icy cold water. [4]

....

....

....

....

*13 **Figure 8** is an illustration of an eye starting to look at a very bright object in the distance.

Figure 8

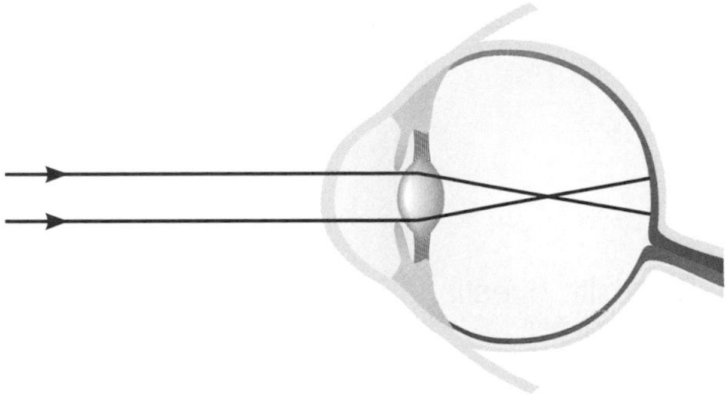

Changes happen inside the eye to get a focused image that does not appear too bright. How will muscles in the eye make these changes? [4]

....

....

....

....

14 **Figure 9** shows a mango. Mangoes are tropical fruits that are exported all over the world. They are picked early and ripened when they reach the UK.

Figure 9

Which method is used to ripen the fruit? Tick (✓) **one** box. [1]

Stored in an atmosphere of carbon dioxide gas ☐

Sprayed with a solution of the hormone auxin ☐

Stored in an atmosphere of ethene gas ☐

Sprayed with a solution of the hormone gibberellin ☐

15 **Figure 10** shows a broad bean seed five days after germination.

Figure 10

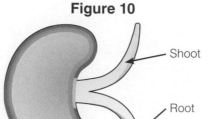

(a) Describe and explain how the shoot responds to gravity. [3]

....

....

....

(b) The root grows in the opposite direction. Describe how auxin behaves in the root. [2]

....

....

16 Two students carried out an experiment to investigate the decay of grass cuttings.

• They put the cuttings in three different-coloured plastic bags – each bag had a few very small holes for ventilation.

• The bags were placed together at the edge of the school field.

• The bags were weighed at the start of the experiment and again three months later.

Table 1 shows the results.

Table 1

	Black bag (A)	Yellow bag (B)	White bag (C)
Mass of bag and grass cuttings at the start (g)	320.4	350.6	325.7
Mass of bag and grass cuttings after three months (g)	271.7	305.7	290.9
% decrease in mass	15.2	12.8	10.7

(a) Predict the percentage decrease in mass if the experiment is repeated with a dark brown bag. Explain your answer. [3]

....

....

....

(b) Putting the three bags in the same place on the school field is controlling a variable.
Suggest **two** other control variables to help improve this experiment. [2]

1. ....

2. ....

17 The reaction times of six people were measured.

They put on headphones and were asked to push a button when they heard a sound. The button was connected to a timer.

Table 2 shows the results.

Table 2

Person	Gender	Reaction time in seconds				
		1	2	3	4	5
A	Male	0.26	0.25	0.27	0.25	0.27
B	Female	0.25	0.25	0.26	0.22	0.24
C	Male	0.31	1.43	0.32	0.29	0.32
D	Female	0.22	0.23	0.25	0.22	0.23
E	Male	0.27	0.31	0.30	0.28	0.26
F	Female	0.23	0.19	0.21	0.21	0.22

(a) Describe a pattern in these results. [1]

....

(b) Calculate the mean reaction time for person C, ignoring any outliers. Show your working. [2]

....

....

(c) When person D was concentrating on the test, someone touched her arm and she jumped.
Her response was a reflex action. What are the **two** main features of a reflex action? [2]

....

....

*(d) A reflex action involves a 'message' travelling along a sensory neurone as an electrical impulse.
The electrical impulse reaches a junction called a synapse.

Describe what happens at the synapse for the 'message' to continue its journey. [4]

....

....

....

....

18 Neuroscientists have linked particular areas of the brain to different functions.

Outline **one** technique used to map the brain and discuss an ethical issue associated with it. **[2]**

....

....

19 **Figure 11** shows hormone levels in a woman's bloodstream during her menstrual cycle.

Figure 11

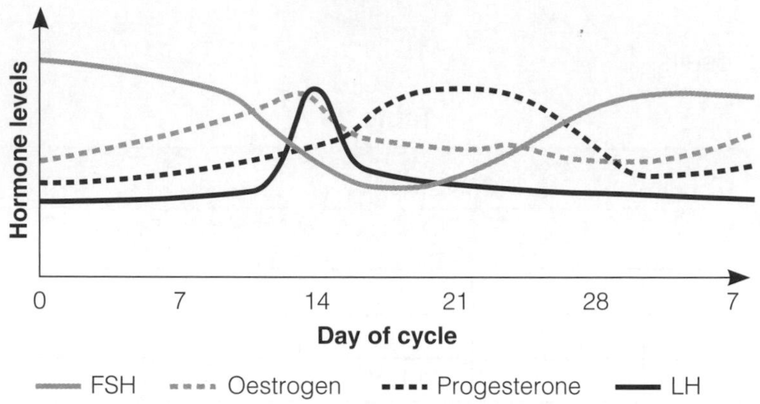

FSH   Oestrogen   Progesterone   LH

(a) The woman believes that her best chance of becoming pregnant is after day 21 of the cycle. Is she correct? Use the levels of hormones in **Figure 11** to explain your answer. **[2]**

....

....

....

(b) What is the role of progesterone in the menstrual cycle? **[2]**

....

....

(c) Explain how the hormones used in oral contraceptives prevent conception. **[2]**

....

....

(d) Fertility drugs have helped many couples have children, where previously they could not. However, the process is not without its problems.

Outline **two** problems with this type of treatment. **[2]**

....

....

20 **Figure 12** shows four methods of plant reproduction.

Figure 12

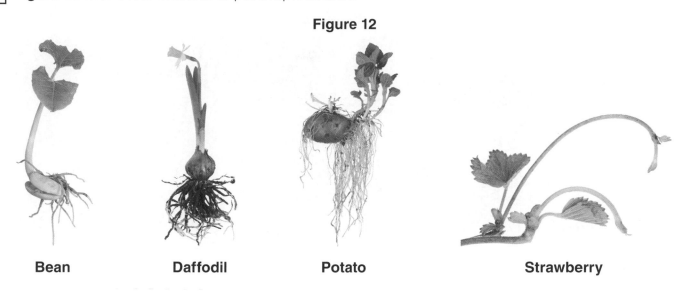

| Bean | Daffodil | Potato | Strawberry |

Which method shows plant reproduction with the greatest genetic variation?
Tick (✓) **one** box. [1]

Bean plant from seed ☐

Daffodil plant from bulb ☐

Potato plant from tuber ☐

Strawberry plant from runner ☐

21 **Figure 13** shows the three stages involved in tissue culturing.

Figure 13

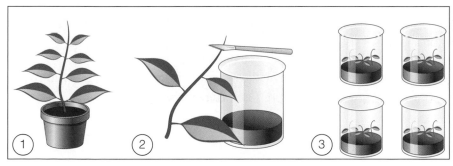

Outline **one** benefit and **one** disadvantage of this method of plant cultivation. [2]

....

....

*22 A farmer keeps two different herds of cows. The two types of cow are shown in **Figure 14**.

Figure 14

Herd 1   Herd 2

- Each cow in herd 1 produces a high volume of low fat milk.

- Each cow in herd 2 produces small amounts of high cream milk.

The farmer wants to modify his milk yield to get high volumes of creamy milk. He can sell the creamy milk to local ice-cream makers.

Describe how the farmer can use selective breeding to achieve his aim. **[4]**

....

....

....

....

23 Selective breeding methods have recently been used to produce vegetables that, when eaten, help reduce cholesterol levels in humans.

If the vegetables had been produced by genetic engineering, some people may be worried about them being used for human consumption. Give **two** reasons why. **[2]**

....

....

....

24 **(a)** Which term describes different versions of the same gene?
Tick (✓) **one** box. **[1]**

Variant ☐

Dominant ☐

Recessive ☐

Allele ☐

(b) Figure 15 shows Max and Sharon with their three children: Dylan, Emily and Georgina.

Figure 15

Max   Sharon

Dylan   Emily   Georgina

Which members of the family share the most genes? Tick (✓) **one** box. [1]

Dylan and Max ☐

Emily and Sharon ☐

Emily and Georgina ☐

Georgina and Max ☐

25 **(a)** DNA contains four bases: G, C, A and T.

There are the same number of G bases as C bases. There are also the same number of A bases as T bases.

The analysis of one strand of DNA found that 27% was composed of base T. Calculate the percentage of the other three bases. Show your working. [3]

....

....

....

(b) The compounds that form the 'rungs' on the DNA ladder and code for the structure of a protein are arranged in pairs.

Figure 16 shows a diagram of DNA. One strand has been filled in.

Figure 16

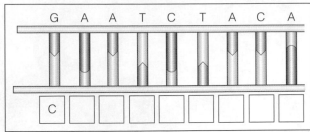

Enter the matching compounds in the boxes. [1]

(c) How many amino acids are coded by the section of DNA shown in **Figure 16**?
Explain your answer. [3]

....

....

....

26 Cystic fibrosis is a genetic disorder. Adam has the disorder but his mother and father did not show signs of the condition.

(a) Complete the Punnett diagram to show how this could occur. Use f as the allele for cystic fibrosis. [2]

(b) Before Adam was conceived, what was the probability that his parents would have a child with cystic fibrosis? [1]

....

(c) Which phrase describes the genotype of Adam's parents? [1]

....

*27 (a) Diabetes is a condition where the body cannot control the level of glucose in the blood.

Describe how the human body normally controls the level of glucose in the blood and how people with type 1 and type 2 diabetes maintain the correct levels of glucose in the blood. **[6]**

....

....

....

....

....

....

....

....

....

....

(b) Diabetes can adversely affect the kidneys.

Kidneys remove urea from the bloodstream. Outline what other jobs the kidneys do. **[2]**

....

....

(c) A person with kidney disease must control their diet to reduce the kidneys' workload.

Explain in detail why the amount of protein in the diet must be limited. **[4]**

....

....

....

....

....

28 Large areas of Amazon rainforest are cleared to provide land for farming every year.
Explain how deforestation is linked to global warming. **[2]**

....

....

....

29 Write down **two** reasons why biodiversity is important. **[2]**

....

....

30 Modern sustainable farming methods can provide enough food for the human population.
Explain the meaning of the phrase 'sustainable farming'. **[1]**

....

TOTAL FOR PAPER = 100 MARKS

Answers

CELL BIOLOGY

Page 4

1. (a) Nucleus **(1)**
    (b) Mitochondria are too small to see with a light microscope / require an electron microscope / resolution of microscope not high enough. **(1)**
    (c) Liver cells require the release of a lot of energy **(1)**; mitochondria release energy for muscle contraction **(1)**.
    (d) Cell, cytoplasm, nucleus, chromosome, gene **(2 marks for everything in the correct order, 1 mark if cell, cytoplasm and nucleus are in the correct order, reading left to right)**

2. (a) Bacteria have a chromosomal loop; have plasmids; no nuclear membrane / nucleus. **(1)**
    (b) Prokaryotic ✓ **(1)**

Page 5

1. (a) An undifferentiated cell that can develop into one of many different types. **(1)**
    (b) **Any two from:** nucleus, cytoplasm, cell / plasma membrane, mitochondria, ribosomes. **(2)**

2. (a) **Any two from:** therapeutic cloning, treating paralysis, repairing nerve damage, cancer research, grow new organs for transplantation. **(2)**
    (b) **Any one from:** stem cells are sometimes obtained from human embryos and people believe it is wrong to use embryos for this purpose, risk of viral infections. **(1)**

3. $\dfrac{3600}{30} \times 200$ **(1)** = 24 000 μm **(1)** = 24 mm **(1)**

Page 6

1. (a) Line should point to one of the objective lenses / rotating nose cone. **(1)**
    (b) The organelles are too small to see **(1)** / microscope doesn't have a high enough resolving power. **(1)**
    (c) Size of real object = $\dfrac{3}{400}$ **(1)** = 0.0075 cm **(1)** = 75 μm **(1)**

2. (a) Scanning electron microscope **(1)**
    (b) **For 2 marks, accept any answer between 80–100 minutes**; if answer is incorrect, award 1 mark for the idea that there have been 4 divisions.

Page 7

1. **Any two from:** specialised organs carry out a specific job; multicellular organisms are complex and require specialised organs so they can grow larger; single-celled organisms are small enough not to require specialised cells and transport systems. **(2)**

2.

Mitosis	Meiosis
Involved in asexual reproduction	**Involved in sexual reproduction (1)**
Produces clones / no variation (1)	Produces variation
Produces cells with 46 chromosomes	**Produces cells with 23 chromosomes (1)**

3. (a) Meiosis **(1)**
    (b) Four cells produced (in second meiotic division) **(1)**

4. **Top label:** New bases pair up with exposed bases on each strand **(1)**; **bottom label:** Two identical strands of DNA / double helices formed **(1)**.

Page 8

1. $C_6H_{12}O_6 + 6O_2 \longrightarrow 6CO_2 + 6H_2O$ **(1 mark for correct formulae, 1 mark for correct balancing)**

2. (a) **Any two from:** larger athletes will use more oxygen due to their higher muscle mass; the adjustment allows rates to be fairly / accurately compared; different athletes may have different masses. **(2)**
    (b) Sprinting has a greater energy demand **(1)**, so more oxygen is needed **(1)**.

    (c) Boris' consumption rate would be lower **(1)** because his lungs, heart and muscles are less efficient at transporting / using oxygen **(1)**.

Page 9

1. (a)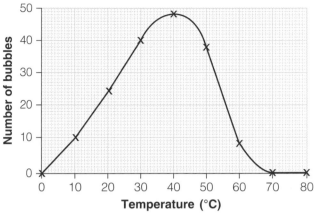

    (2 marks for correct plotting; 1 mark for smooth curve; subtract 1 mark for every incorrect plot)
    (b) The rate of bubbles produced increases until it reaches an optimum / maximum **(1)**; then it decreases rapidly, producing no bubbles at 70°C **(1)**.
    (c) 40°C **(1)**
    (d) **Any two from:** enzyme / active site has changed shape / become denatured; substrate / hydrogen peroxide no longer fits active site, so substrate cannot be broken down; low pH of the stomach **or** amylase works best at alkaline pH and stomach is acid. **(2)**

TRANSPORT SYSTEMS AND PHOTOSYNTHESIS

Page 10

1. (a) **Any two named small nutrient molecules**, e.g. glucose, vitamins, minerals, ions, amino acids, oxygen **(2)**.
    (b) **Any one from:** carbon dioxide or urea. **(1)**

2. (a) Water moves down concentration gradient from high water concentration to low water concentration **(1)**, across a partially / differentially permeable membrane / plasma membrane **(1)**; gradient maintained by input and output of water at each end of cell line **(1)**.
    (b) Water moving from plant cell to plant cell ✓ **(1)**; A pear losing water in a concentrated solution of sugar ✓ **(1)**; Water moving from blood plasma to body cells ✓ **(1)**.

3. (a) Rhubarb cells turgid **(1)**; because water moves into cells due to osmosis **(1)**.
    (b) **Any two from:** plasmolysed; plant cell vacuole extremely small; membrane pulled away from wall. **(2)**

Page 11

1. **From top: (a)** (upper) epidermis **(1)**; **(b)** spongy layer / mesophyll **(1)**; **(c)** air space **(1)**.

2. **Roots:** anchor plant in soil / absorb water and minerals **(1)**
    Stem: supports leaves and flowers, transports substances up and down the plant **(1)**
    Leaf: organs of photosynthesis **(1)**
    Flower: reproductive organs, formation of seeds **(1)**

3. **Any three from:** dead cells without cytoplasm; no end walls; hollow lumen; continuous tubes – all adaptations allow efficient movement of water in columns. **(3)**

4. (a) **Any one from:** phloem have perforated end walls / xylem has no end wall; xylem have hard cell walls (contain lignin) / phloem have soft cell walls. **(1)**
    (b) Aphids extract / eat sugar **(1)**; sugar solution transported in phloem **(1)**.

Page 12

1. (a) $\frac{8}{43} \times 100 = 18.6\%$ **(1 mark for calculation, 1 mark for correct answer)**

    (b) B (cold moving air) **(1)**

    (c) Water column in xylem would move upwards / towards the leaves more quickly. **(1)**

2. **This is a model answer, which would score the full 6 marks:** As light intensity increases during the day, the rate of photosynthesis increases in the guard cells. This results in more sugar being manufactured, which raises the solute concentration. Increased potassium ions contribute to increased solute concentration too. The guard cells therefore draw in water from surrounding cells by osmosis, becoming more turgid. This causes the stoma to become wider. The arrangement of cellulose in the cell walls of the guard cells means that there is more expansion in the outer wall, resulting in a wider stoma.

Page 13

1. (a) (i) Scotland **(1)**

    (ii) 50 deaths per 100 000 (210 − 160) **(1)**

    (b) Men have higher death rates than women. **(1)**

2. Artery – 3 **(1)**; Capillaries in the body – 4 **(1)**; Vein – 1 **(1)**; Capillaries in the lungs – 2 **(1)**

Page 14

1. (a) 924.5 **(2)**; **if the answer is incorrect then showing the working** (926 + 923 = 1849, then $\frac{1849}{2}$) **will gain 1 mark**

    (b) Rats have different body masses / to standardise results. **(1)**

    (c) As the warfarin dose increases, the time to clot also increases. **(1)**

2. Agree **(1)** because as vital capacity increases the time underwater also increases **(1)**.

    Or disagree **(1)** due to **any one from:** only five subjects / not enough data; need to find divers with higher / lower vital capacities **(1)**.

Page 15

1. (a)

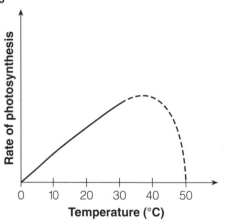

Temperature (°C) **(1)**

    (b) As the temperature increases, the rate of photosynthesis increases due to more rapid molecular movement and therefore more frequent successful collisions between molecules **(1)**. By 40 °C, the rate peaks and beyond this point enzymes controlling photosynthesis become denatured and the reaction stops **(1)**.

2. (a) Leaves **(1)**

    (b) **Cellulose:** cell walls for support **(1)**; **Protein:** growth / cell membranes / enzyme production **(1)**.

    (c) carbon dioxide + water ⟶ glucose + oxygen
    (1 mark for reactants, 1 mark for products)

3. (a) **Any two from:** the increased temperature from the stove will increase photosynthesis rate; increased carbon dioxide concentration will have the same effect; increased photosynthesis means increased starch production / yield. **(2)**

    (b) **Any one from:** increase light regime, e.g. artificial lighting switched on at night time; increased light intensity / brighter lights. **(1)**

HEALTH, DISEASE AND THE DEVELOPMENT OF MEDICINES

Page 16

1. (a) 13.8–14.8% **(1)**

    (b) Glycogen **(1)** found in liver / muscles **(1)**

    (c) **Any two from:** heart disease / CVD / stroke; cancer; diabetes; asthma / eczema / autoimmune diseases; poor nutrition – named example, e.g. rickets; genetic conditions, e.g. cystic fibrosis; eating disorders, e.g. anorexia; mental health conditions; alcoholism / addiction; named inherited disease. **(2)**

2. (a) ×20 **(1)**

    (b) **Any one from:** low birth weight; premature birth; higher risk of still birth. **(1)**

Page 17

1. (a) Pathogen **(1)**

    (b) Cause cell damage **(1)**; the toxins produced damage tissues. **(1)**

2. (a) **Any two from:** diarrhoea; vomiting; dehydration. **(2)**

    (b) Cholera spread by drinking contaminated water **(1)**; water easily contaminated because water supply / sewage systems damaged **or** overcrowding and poor hygiene in disaster zones **(1)**.

3. (a) **Any two from:** malaria is transmitted by the mosquito; warm temperatures are ideal for mosquitos to thrive; stagnant water is an ideal habitat for mosquito eggs to be laid / larvae to survive **(2)**.

    (b) **Mosquito:** vector **(1)**
    Plasmodium: parasite **(1)**

    (c) Nets will deter mosquitoes / prevent bites / prevent transferral of plasmodium **(1)**; antivirals are ineffective as plasmodium is a protist / not a virus **(1)**.

Page 18

1. (a) Antibodies **(1)**

    (b) Pathogens are clumped together to prevent their further reproduction, to make them easier for phagocytes to digest. **(1)**

    (c)

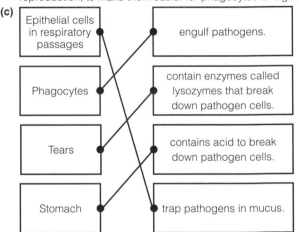

(1 mark for each correct line up to 3 marks, subtract 1 mark for any additional lines)

2. (a) **Any one from:** droplet infection / coughing / sneezing / water droplets in breath / aerosol. **(1)**

    (b) Answer in the range 16–17 days **(1)**

    (c) 9 arbitrary units **(1)** (9.5 – 0.5) **(1)**

    (d) Memory cells recognise future invasion of pathogen **(1)**; they can produce the necessary antibodies much quicker, and at higher levels, if the same pathogen is detected again **(1)**.

Page 19

1. **This is a model answer, which would score the full 6 marks:** HIV proteins can be triggered and manufactured in existing human cells. The genes that code for the viral proteins are injected into the bloodstream. An adenovirus shell prevents them from being destroyed by the body's general defences. Once inside a cell, the genes instruct it to produce viral proteins that are presented at the cell surface membrane. The body's lymphocytes then recognise these antigens and produce antibodies against them. Memory cells sensitive to the viral proteins are then stored in case the body is exposed to the antigens again.

2. **Accept any three from:** Bacteria are becoming resistant to many modern antibiotics; doctors have in the past over-prescribed antibiotics; mutations in bacteria have led to resistant strains developing; some people don't complete the course of antibiotics. **(3)**

Page 20

1. **(a) Any two from:** to ensure that the drug is actually effective / more effective than placebo; to work out the most effective dose / method of application; to comply with legislation. **(2)**
   (b) Double blind trials involve volunteers who are randomly allocated to groups – neither they nor the doctors / scientists know if they have been given the new drug or a placebo **(1)**; this eliminates all bias from the test **(1)**.
   (c) (i) Total patients = 226; $\frac{21}{226} \times 100$ **(1)** = 9.29% **(1)**
   (ii) Yes, there are more patients who took the drug and had a cardiovascular event than those who took the placebo. However, there is not a large difference between the groups. **(1)** No, the cardiovascular events could include other conditions apart from heart attacks. **(1)**
   (iii) Rash **(1)**; the difference in numbers of patients who got a rash between the alketronol and placebo groups is quite large **(1)**.

Page 21

1. **(a) Mineral deficiency:** lack of nitrates **(1) Leaf appearance:** yellow leaves and stunted growth **(1)** (Also accept **Mineral deficiency:** lack of magnesium / potassium / phosphate **(1)**; **Leaf appearance:** chlorosis / discolouration of the leaves **(1)**)
   (b) There is a high concentration of *Chalara* cases in the East of England ✓ **(1)**
   (c) (i) Any two from: burning trees destroys fungus / *Chalara*; prevents further spores being produced; reduces spread of spores. **(2)**
   (ii) Any one from: not all trees removed; trees may produce spores before being detected / destroyed; more spores could be introduced by wind from mainland Europe. **(1)**

COORDINATION AND CONTROL

Page 22

1. homeostasis **(1)**; receptors **(1)**; effectors **(1)**
2. **(a)** Negative feedback **(1)**
   (b) (i) It reduces production of ACTH. **(1)**
   (ii) Any one from: ineffective nutrient distribution; inability to reduce inflammation; inefficient water control. **(1)**
   (iii) Patient D **(1)**
   (iv) 5 × 7 = 35 μg per litre **(2 marks for correct answer; if answer is incorrect, 1 mark for showing working)**

Page 23

1. **(a)** Nucleus **(1)**; **(b)** Cell body / cytoplasm **(1)**
2. **(a)** Brain **(1)**
   (b) A means of detecting external stimuli, i.e. a **receptor (1)**; transferral of electrical impulses to the CNS, i.e. a **sensory neurone (1)**; a coordinator / control system, i.e. a **brain (1)**.
3. **(a)** Synapse **(1)**
   (b) Any three from: transmitter substance released at end of first neurone in response to impulse; travels across synapse by diffusion; transmitter binds with receptor molecules on next neurone; nervous impulse released in second neurone **(3)**.

Page 24

1. **(a)** Cerebral cortex / cerebrum **(1)**
   (b) The brain contains junctions between all three types of neurone ✓ **(1)**
   The brain is part of the central nervous system ✓ **(1)**.
2. **(a) Any two from:** muscle contraction; generates heat; through respiration. **(2)**
   (b) Any two from: evaporation of sweat from skin; requires heat from body; radiation; endothermic change. **(2)**
   (c) 37 °C **(1)**

(d) Blood vessels / arterioles narrow **(1)**; blood shunted below adiposetissue / fat layer **(1)**; fat insulation reduces heat loss from blood. **(1)**

Page 25

1. **(a)** A3 **(1)**; B1 **(1)**; C2 **(1)**; D4 **(1)**
   (b) Light rays fall on the **cornea** where they are refracted / bent **(1)**; the **lens** then refracts / bends light further **(1)**.
2. Caused by an eyeball that is too long / weak suspensory ligaments that cannot pull the lens into a thin shape **(1)**; corrected using a concave lens **(1)**.
3. Bobcats are likely to be able to form more detailed images in bright light / have better colour vision **(1)**; because cone density is greater **(1)**; cannot conclude that they have better night vision as data about rods is not available **(1)**.

Page 26

1. **Gland:** pancreas **(1)**   **Hormone:** insulin / glucagon **(1)**
2. **(a) Any two from:** after meal, a rise in glucose levels will be detected by device; which will cause hormone implant to release insulin; insulin released to bring blood glucose level down. **(2)**
   (b) People with type 2 diabetes can often control their sugar level by adjusting their diet **(1)**; body's cells often no longer respond to insulin **(1)**.
3.

Gland	Hormones produced
Pituitary gland	**TSH, ADH, LH** and **FSH** (accept any two)
Pancreas	Insulin and glucagon
Thyroid gland	Thyroxine
Adrenal gland	Adrenaline
Ovary	**Oestrogen** and **progesterone**
Testes	Testosterone

(1 mark for each correct line)

Page 27

1. **(a)** 1600 ml **(1)**
   (b) Amounts are equal **(1)**; important that water intake should balance water output to avoid dehydration **(1)**.
   (c) Intake of water greater **(1)**; output from sweating greater **(1)**; water gained from respiration greater **(1)**, as muscles contracting more / respiring more **(1)**.
2. **(a)** B **(1)**
   (b) C **(1)**
   (c) A **(1)**
   (d) Low water levels in blood detected by receptors / in blood vessels / in brain **(1)**; more ADH released by pituitary gland **(1)**; acts on collecting duct / kidney **(1)**; which is stimulated to absorb more water back into bloodstream **(1)**.

Page 28

1. Days 5–14: uterus wall is being repaired **(1)**; egg released at approximately 14 days from ovary **(1)**; days 14–28: uterus lining maintained **(1)**.
2.

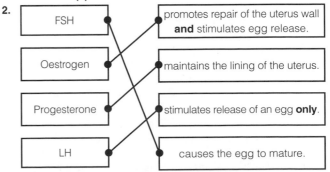

(1 mark for each correct line up to 3 marks)

3. (a) Negative feedback **(1)**
  (b) FSH **(1)**
  (c) Progesterone **(1)**
  (d) Continues to be produced **(1)** in large quantities / at high levels **(1)**.

Page 29
1. (a) Leroy and Jane **(1)**
  (b) Three: Tim and Margaret, Rohit and Saleema, and Leroy and Jane. **(1)**
  (c) Although irregular ovulation has a lower success rate **(1)**; it affects over twice as many couples (16 × 75 produces a larger total than 7 × 95). **(1)**
  (d) Both methods mean that Jane does not make any genetic contribution **(1)**; egg donation has a high rate of success but can be expensive **(1)**; surrogacy might be cheaper but there is a risk that the surrogate mother might develop an attachment to the baby / want to keep it **(1)**; egg donation requires invasive technique **(1)**.
2. Any two from: the contraceptive pill contains hormones that inhibit FSH production; e.g. oestrogen / progesterone; eggs therefore fail to mature; progesterone causes production of sticky cervical mucus that hinders movement of sperm **(2)**.

Page 30
1. The shoot grows upwards and root grows downwards when the bean germinates **(1)**; after it is turned, the shoot shows negative geotropism / gravitropism and grows upwards **(1)**; the root shows positive geotropism / gravitropism and grows in same direction as force of gravity **(1)**.
2. Plant hormones ✓ **(1)**
3. This is a model answer, which would score the full 6 marks:
Miriam would take 50 seeds, all of the same mass and planted at the same time. These would be grown in the same compost in a large tray with an equal spacing of 5 cm between each seed. The seeds would be placed in an enclosed chamber with a single lamp source shining from one direction. A similar tray could be placed in a chamber where the light was entering uniformly from all directions. This would be the control. Over the next five days, the compost in both trays would be supplied with a known dose of water to ensure that it was kept moist. At the end of a five-day period, the seeds that have now grown shoots would be removed. A count would be made of the number of shoots that were leaning significantly away from the vertical towards the source of light. It would be expected that Miriam would find that most, if not all, of the shoots were pointing towards the light in the first tray, whereas the shoots in the second tray would be growing vertically. This procedure could be repeated numerous times to increase the reliability of the observations. **The answer provides all possible detail and alternatives to answer the question. In summary, you need to cover:** fair testing / controlled experiment; how the number of responding seedlings would be measured; the correct pattern in the results.

INHERITANCE, VARIATION AND EVOLUTION
Page 31
1. gametes **(1)**; haploid **(1)**; meiosis **(1)**
2. Meiosis shuffles genes, which makes each gamete unique ✓ **(1)**; Gametes fuse randomly ✓ **(1)**
3. (a) Any three from: sexual reproduction can be an advantage to a species if the environment changes; asexual reproduction is more advantageous when the environment is not changing; some organisms use both types of reproduction, therefore both have their advantages; sexual reproduction might yield disadvantageous adaptations in an individual when the environment changes. **(3)**
  (b) Sexual: male and female parents required; slower than asexual; requires meiosis; more resources (e.g. time, energy) required. **Asexual:** only one parent required; faster than sexual; requires mitosis only; less resources required. **(1)**
  (c) Cytoplasm and organelles duplicated **(1)**; as a 'bud' **(1)**

Page 32
1. The genome of an organism is the entire genetic material present in its adult body cells ✓ **(1)**; The HGP involved collaboration between US and UK geneticists ✓ **(1)**; The project allowed genetic abnormalities to be tracked between generations ✓ **(1)**.
2. (a) Organisms with very similar features / chimpanzee and human share equal DNA coding for protein A. **(1)**
  (b) Yeast **(1)**
3. (a) Any two from: warn women about the risk of cancer ahead of time; enable early and regular screening; enable early treatment; suggest treatment that is targeted. **(2)**
  (b) Other factors may contribute to onset of cancer **(1)**; risk is in terms of a probability (which is not 100%) **(1)**.

Page 33
1. (a) T pairs with A; C pairs with G **(both correct for 1 mark)**
  (b) 3 **(1)**
2. (a) Any two from: UV light; radioactive substances; X-rays; certain chemicals / mutagens. **(2)**
  (b) Base / codon / triplet sequence changed **(1)**; leads to change in amino acid sequence **(1)**; protein no longer has correct shape to perform its job **(1)**.
3. Stage 1: DNA unzips and exposes the bases on each strand / a molecule of messenger RNA (mRNA) is constructed from one of these template strands. **(1)**
Stage 2: The mRNA carries a complementary version of the gene / travels out of the nucleus to the cytoplasm. **(1)**
Stage 3: In the ribosome, the mRNA is 'read' / tRNA molecules carry individual amino acids to add to a growing protein (polypeptide). **(1)**
Stage 4: The new polypeptide folds into a unique shape / is released into the cytoplasm. **(1)**

Page 34
1. (a) 39 **(1)**
  (b) Black is the dominant gene / allele; white is recessive **(1) (no marks given for references to 'black chromosome' or 'white chromosome')**; the allele for black fur is passed on / inherited from the father **(1)**.
  (c) Correct genotype or gametes for both parents (Bb and bb) **(1)**; genotype of offspring correct (Bb and bb) **(1)**; correct phenotype of offspring **(1)**.

	b	b
B	Bb Black	Bb Black
b	bb White	bb White

Or

B   b   b   b

Bb   Bb   bb   bb

Black   Black   White   White

2. (a)

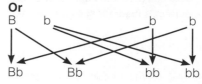

Brown eyes   ×   Blue eyes

Parents   BB   ×   bb

Gametes   B   B   b   b

Offspring   Bb   Bb   Bb   Bb

Phenotype   Brown   Brown   Brown   Brown

(1 mark will be awarded for the phenotype row and 1 mark for offspring row.)

(b)

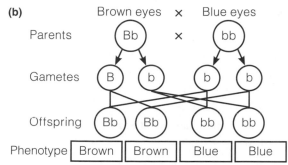

(1 mark will be awarded for the phenotype row and 1 mark for the offspring row.)

Page 35

1. (a) 205–215 million years ago **(1)**
    (b) (i) Cretaceous **(1)**
        (ii) They have discovered fossils. **(1)**
    (c) Lizard **(1)**
    (d) Archosaur **(1)**

Page 36

1. (a)

Before Industrial Revolution		After Industrial Revolution	
Pale	**Dark**	**Pale**	**Dark**
1260	107	89	1130

(1 mark for mean numbers before Industrial Revolution; 1 mark for mean numbers after Industrial Revolution)

    (b)

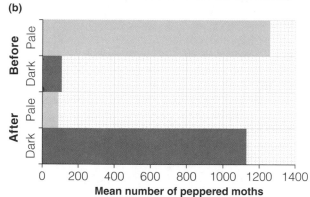

(2 marks for correct plotting of bars; subtract 1 mark for every incorrect plot.)

    (c) The pale-coloured moths could camouflage themselves easily against the silver birch tree bark. **(1)**
    (d) Dark-coloured peppered moths were more camouflaged than pale moths after the Industrial Revolution due to the effects of air pollution **(1)**; dark moths had an increased chance of survival and consequently an increased chance of reproducing and passing on genes **(1)**.
2. Lucy was one of the earliest known hominids to have an upright stance. **(1)**

Page 37

1. evolved; slow; adapted; genes **(4 words correct = 2 marks, 2 or 3 words correct = 1 mark, 1 or 0 words correct = 0 marks)**
2. Mendel's work showed that characteristics could be passed on from parents to offspring; studies of genetic material have revealed the unit of inheritance as the gene / DNA **(1)**.
3. (a) Mitosis **(1)**
    (b) It enables them to produce many plants with the same desired characteristics from just one parent plant **(1)**; it enables them to produce many plants quickly. **(1)**
    (c) If plants are susceptible to a disease or change, all the plants with those genes will be affected **(1)**; reduction in genetic variation reduces potential for further selective breeding **(1)**.

4. **Any one from:** embryos can develop into healthy human beings and the rights of the embryo / potential life have to be addressed; at some stage the embryo is able to suffer pain and at this point it would be unethical to experiment on it. **(1)**

Page 38

1. (a) **Any three from:** Allow chosen males and females to mate / breed / reproduce together; select offspring from several matings that have high quality wool; allow these sheep to mate together; repeat the process over many generations **(stages must be in sequence)**. **(3)**
    (b) **Any one from:** high quality meat / lamb; thick coat; hardiness / ability to withstand harsh winters; colouration / markings; disease resistance. **(1)**
2. **Any two from:** involves genes, not whole organisms; genes transferred from one organism to another; much more precise in terms of passing on characteristics; rapid production; cheaper than selective breeding; (or reverse argument). **(2)**
3. (a) Crops containing soya can be sprayed with herbicide so weeds are killed rather than soya. **(1)**
    (b) Rice produces carotene, which provides poor populations with vitamin A. **(1)**
4. GM plants may cross-breed with wild plants, resulting in wild plants / weeds that are herbicide-resistant. **(1)**

Page 39

1. (a) **Underline any one of the following**; carnivorous big cats; five toes on their front paws and four toes on their back paws; claws can be drawn back. **(1)**
    (b) Leopards are more closely related to tigers **(1)**; both are the Panthera genus / snow leopards are a different genus **(1)**.
2. (a) Possesses features that are found in reptiles and birds **(1)**; feathers place it with birds but it also has teeth / does not have a beak like reptiles – it is an intermediate form **(1)**.

ECOSYSTEMS

Page 40

1. features; characteristics **(either way round for features or characteristics)**; suited; environment; evolutionary; survival **(6 words correct = 3 marks, 4 or 5 words correct = 2 marks, 2 or 3 words correct = 1 mark, 1 or 0 words correct = 0 marks)**
2. (a)

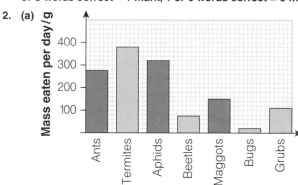

(2 marks for correctly plotting bars, 1 mark for correctly labelling x axis.)

    (b) $\frac{380}{1330} \times 100 = 28.6\%$
    (1 mark for correct answer, 1 mark for showing working)
    (c) It occupies more than one habitat / niche **(1)**; eats a wide variety of food / prey **(1)**.

Page 41

1. (a) Habitat **(1)**
    (b) Ecosystem **(1)**
    (c) **Any one from:** pooter; sweepnet; light trap. **(1)**
    (d) $16 \times 4 \times 5000 = 320\,000$ **(1 mark for correct answer, 1 mark for showing working)**
    (e) (i) Less competition for food between beetles **(1)**; numbers increase as a result **(1)**.
        (ii) Snail numbers would decline. **(1)**

Page 42

1. (a) Biogas **(1)**
   (b) **Any two from:** burned to generate electricity; burned to produce hot water / steam / for central heating; used as fuel in houses; used for cooking. **(2)**
   (c) Remote areas don't have access to mains electricity; burning biogas can generate electricity. **(1)**
2. (a) Tube D **(1)**; because it is warm and moist **(1)**.
   (b) The soil / air / surface of the leaf **(1)**
   (c) So that air / oxygen can get in **(1)**
   (d) **Accept one from:** they could count the number of whole discs left at the end; they could record what fraction / percentage of leaf discs decayed and find an average; they could measure the percentage decrease in mass of discs by measuring mass before and after time in soil. **(1)**

Page 43

1. Water; wind; wood **(1)**
2. **Climate zones** shift, causing ecosystems and habitats to change; organisms are displaced and become extinct. **(1) Sea levels** rise, causing flooding of coastal regions; islands are inundated and disappear beneath sea level. **(1) Ice caps and glaciers** melt and retreat, resulting in loss of habitat. **(1)**
3. (a) See graph **(2)**
   (b) Millions (Also accept billions) **(1)**

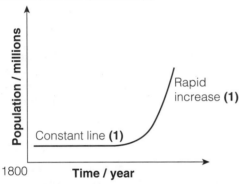

   (c) **Any two from:** insufficient birth control; better life expectancy; better health care; better hygienic practice. **(2)**

Page 44

1. **Any two from:** climate change; new predators; habitat destruction; hunting; competition; pollution. **(2)**
2. (a) Cutting down large areas of forest ✓ **(1)**
   (b) Increase in atmospheric carbon dioxide ✓ **(1)**

3. **Any two from:** provide land for agriculture; road building; mining; construction. **(2)**
4. tropical; trees; carbon dioxide; biodiversity; extinct; habitats **(6)**
5. Nutrients in the soil are absorbed by crops and are not replaced. **(1)**

Page 45

1. (a) Chemical energy ✓ **(1)**
   (b) $\dfrac{1000}{6000} \times 100 = 16.7\%$
   (2 marks for correct answer; if answer incorrect, allow 1 mark for $\dfrac{1000}{6000} \times 100$)
   (c) Cellulose in plant material requires more energy to digest **(1)**; so larger amounts need to be consumed **(1)**. Accept converse argument for humans.
   (d) **This is a model answer, which would score the full 6 marks:** Shorter food chains are more energy-efficient because they have fewer trophic levels. A vegetarian food chain may have only two levels: plants – humans, whereas a meat-eating diet will have three or more. We know that energy is lost at each trophic level as respiration, heat, excretion, egestion and movement. In this way, a consumer may lose up to 90% energy and only pass on 10% to the next consumer in the chain. Producing food for a vegetarian population requires decreased areas of land because at least one trophic level is removed from the food chain. A field of wheat will feed many more humans than a field of cattle. This can be seen in a pyramid of biomass, where the width of the human trophic level is greater when humans are a primary consumer compared with when they are a secondary or tertiary consumer.

Page 46

1. (a) 160 thousand tonnes (plus or minus 10 000 or in range 150–170) **(1)**
   (b) Overall decrease in numbers **(1)**; temporary rises in 1988–1993 and 2003–2006 **(1)**.
   (c) (i) 1907 tonnes **(1)**
       (ii) Numbers of haddock still declining **(1)**; therefore less fish should be caught in order for fish stocks to recover **(1)**.
   (d) **Any one from:** increasing mesh size to allow young cod to reach breeding age; increase quotas of other fish species. **(1)**

Question number		Answer	Notes	Marks
1	(a)	Lactic acid		1
	(b)	Carbon dioxide		1
2	(a)	Her muscles can release more energy.		1
	(b)	**Cause:** build-up of lactic acid (in muscles)		1
		Recovery: heavy breathing / panting		1
		over a period of time		1
	(c)	**Any three from:** More blood to the muscles. More oxygen supplied to muscles. Increased energy transfer in muscles. More lactic acid to be removed from muscles.		3
3		cell, tissue, organ, system		1
4		White blood cells		1
5	(a)	Right ventricle		1
	(b)	Blood is pumped at a higher pressure. / Blood is pumped a greater distance.		1
	(c)	They stop the backflow of blood.	Allow: they stop blood flowing in the wrong direction.	1
	(d)	$\dfrac{22\,100}{105\,650} \times 100 = 20.91812\%$		1
		21% to two significant figures		1
	(e)	**Any two from:** Low(er) fat intake Low(er) salt intake Regular exercise Healthy body weight Low stress levels		2
6	(a)	It's a physical barrier – prevents pathogens from entering.		1
		It produces antimicrobial secretions (peptides) to kill microorganisms.		1
	(b)	640		1

<table>
<thead>
<tr><th>Time</th><th>Bacteria</th></tr>
</thead>
<tbody>
<tr><td>0</td><td>10</td></tr>
<tr><td>20</td><td>20</td></tr>
<tr><td>40</td><td>40</td></tr>
<tr><td>60</td><td>80</td></tr>
<tr><td>80</td><td>160</td></tr>
<tr><td>100</td><td>320</td></tr>
<tr><td>120</td><td>640</td></tr>
</tbody>
</table>

Question number		Answer	Notes	Marks
			Allow 1 mark for: number doubles six times in two hours.	1
	(c)	Measles is caused by a virus.		1
		Antibiotics only treat bacterial infections.		1
	(d)	$\dfrac{10}{5000} = 0.002 \times 1000$		1
		$= 2\ \mu m$		1
	(e)	**Any two from:** Boil / sterilise all water. Isolate infected individuals. Any basic hygiene measure involving water.	Allow: wash hands / toilets away from water supply, etc.	2
	(f)	There is less chance of contracting the disease as it reduces possible contact with infected people.		1
		The disease cannot spread as people are immune.		1
7		Cell wall		1

8		**Any four from:** Sterilise wire / inoculating loop in flame. Transfer sample of pond water to agar. Seal lid with a cross of tape. Turn upside down (to stop condensation). Incubate at 25 °C.		4
9	(a)	Moral / religious / ethical reasons (e.g. use of embryos to obtain stem cells, it interferes with natural processes, 'plays God' or is against religious beliefs) Possibility of virus transfer		1 1
	(b)	Differentiation		1
10	(a)	**Any two from:** Guard cells fill with water by osmosis. Guard cells change shape. Guard cells become turgid.		2
	(b)	The net movement of particles from an area in which there is a high concentration to one of low concentration. **Any one from:** The (random / net) movement of particles. Particles spread out / particles mix up.	Allow molecules instead of particles.	1 1
11	(a)	**Any two from:** Long Thin Tubes / hollow / no end walls		2
	(b)	**Any two from:** Thin cell wall Large surface area Long, hair-like structure		2
12	(a)	To stop evaporation (of the water)		1
	(b)	2.5 cm³ per day $\frac{50 - 40}{4}$	Allow 1 mark for: total volume lost = 10 cm³	1 1
13	(a)	39		1
	(b)	Mitosis **Any two from:** Chromosomes are copied. Two full sets of chromosomes are made. Each set moves to the opposite end of the cell. **Any one from:** Cell divides in two. Each new cell contains a complete set.		1 2 1
14		Bacteria reproduce very quickly. They form clones / exact copies of the DNA. Bacteria DNA is easily altered / plasmids easily modified.		1 1 1
15		**Any three from:** Smoking Obesity Viruses UV exposure Excessive alcohol intake		3
16	(a)	Amylase		1
	(b)	(Plant) protein broken down by enzymes / protease into amino acids. Amino acids reassembled into new protein.	Allow 1 mark for: 'by enzymes' for reassembly if not credited for breaking down.	1 1 1 1
	(c)	Enzymes are denatured at 60 °C. So proteins / fats from food are not broken down.		1 1
17		**Any three from:** Starch – for storage Fat / oil – for storage Cellulose – to make cell walls Amino acids – to make protein	To score a mark, both the substance and reason must be noted.	3

18	Water has moved / diffused into sugar solution		1
	from a dilute to a more concentrated solution.		1
	Visking tubing is partially permeable.		1
19	Make up 'acid rain' solution (e.g. a dilute sulfuric acid or nitric acid solution, or a solution with a pH in the range 2–6).		1
	Minimum of two groups of infected roses – spray one group of roses with acid solution.		1
	Control variable, e.g. same place in garden.		1
20	Stops it from being eaten		1
21 (a)	Less growth / growth will be stunted		1
(b)	**Advantage** – good supply of nitrate		1
	Disadvantage – large number of rabbits needed to obtain enough manure to treat field		1
22 (a)	Higher temperature leads to faster growth.		1
	More carbon dioxide leads to faster growth.		1
(b)	$6H_2O$		1
	$6O_2$		1
(c)	**Level 3:** Correct patterns for linking both temperature and distance to *rate* of photosynthesis. Explanations linked to light intensity, energy and enzymes.		5–6
	Level 2: One correct pattern / prediction outlined for both distance and temperature. One correct explanation linked to one pattern / prediction.		3–4
	Level 1: One correct pattern / prediction outlined for either distance or temperature. One correct explanation linked to the pattern / prediction.		1–2
	No relevant content		0
	Indicative content **Patterns / predictions** • Fewer bubbles / less photosynthesis with increasing distance • More bubbles at 35 °C • Fewer / no bubbles at 55 °C • Rate of photosynthesis decreases with increasing distance • Rate of photosynthesis increases with temperature up to around 45 °C • Photosynthesis stops at higher temperature **Explanations** • Increase in distance reduces the amount of light • Less light, less photosynthesis • Higher temperature up to around 45 °C – more photosynthesis • More energy increases photosynthesis • Rate of photosynthesis decreases with decrease in light intensity • Correct mention of inverse square law • Rate of photosynthesis increases with increasing energy • Above 45 °C enzymes are denatured and so little or no photosynthesis		
23 (a)	B		1
(b)	The pathogen is disabled / dead / weakened.		1
24	**Any two from:** Viruses are found inside cells. Damaging a virus also damages cells. Viruses have a high mutation rate.		2
25 (a)	Enzymes are proteins.		1
	Monoclonal antibodies target one specific binding site on the enzyme.		1
	The activity is reduced because the binding site on the enzyme is blocked.		1
(b)	**How:** Use of a placebo with some patients.		1
	Why: Removes any bias that may be present in a blind trial, where the doctors know who has the placebo drug.		1
	This is because no one knows who has the real drug.		1

Question Number	Answer	Notes	Marks
1	A		1
2	Disease		1
3	**Any two from:** Small ears (reduce heat loss) Thick fur (reduces heat loss) Thick fat / blubber (reduces heat loss) Sharp claws (for holding onto prey) Hair on pads of feet (to grip ice)		2
4	$\frac{15 \times 21}{4} = 78.75$ 79 (nearest whole number)		1 1
5 (a)	**Any one advantage from:** Ability to control temperature. Ability to control food / high protein food. Easy to catch. It is sustainable. **Any one problem from:** Disease spreads easily. Attracts fish predators. People have ethical objections to this method.		1 1
(b)	Fishing quotas Control of net sizes		1 1
6 (a)	*Strigops*		1
(b)	Primary consumer		1
(c)	**Any three from:** Evolution needs mutations to occur. Mutations are rare. Mutations are usually harmful. Advantageous characteristics are not always selected for. Time is needed for even small changes to occur.		3
7	Less resistant bacteria are killed first / survival of the fittest. If course not completed, resistant bacteria survive. Resistant bacteria then reproduce.		1 1 1
8	The method of formation of other types of rock destroys the remains of the organisms.	Allow specific examples: e.g. the high temperature of igneous rocks destroys the remains.	1
9	**Any two from:** There was not enough evidence at the time. The mechanism through which variation was passed on was not known. It challenged religious beliefs.		2
10	Control of movement		1
11	D		1
12	As body heats up: sweat is produced blood vessels dilate / vasodilation. As the body cools rapidly in the icy cold water: sweating stops / shivering starts blood vessels contract / vasoconstriction / hairs stand up.		2 2
13	Muscles change the shape of the iris. Pupil smaller / less light into eye. Muscles stretch lens. Light focused on retina / back of eye.		1 1 1 1
14	Stored in an atmosphere of ethene gas		1
15 (a)	Shoot grows against gravity / negative geotropism / negative gravitropism. Auxin / growth hormone on lower side of shoot. Lower cells elongate / grow more.		1 1 1
(b)	Inhibits cell growth / reduces growth on lower side of root.		1 1

16	(a)	Any figure in the range 12.9–15.		1
		Trend – darker colour to more mass loss.		1
		Darker colour – higher temperature / faster decay.		1
	(b)	**Any two from:**		
		Grass from same place		
		Same mass of grass cuttings in each bag		
		Same material for bag		
		Same thickness of material for bag		
		Same thickness / packing of material in the bag		2
17	(a)	Female reaction time better than male / females have faster reaction time than males.		1
	(b)	$\dfrac{0.31 + 0.32 + 0.29 + 0.32}{4}$		1
		Answer is 0.31		1
	(c)	Rapid / fast		1
		Automatic / done without thinking		1
	(d)	Impulse causes release of chemical / neurotransmitter from ends of sensory neurone.		1
		Chemical / neurotransmitter diffuses across gap.		1
		Chemical / neurotransmitter binds to receptor molecules on next / relay neurone.		1
		This triggers electrical impulse in next / relay neurone.		1
18		**Any one from:**	Accept other types of scan:	
		MRI scan	e.g. TMS, EEG.	
		Electrically stimulating brain		
		Study of people with brain damage		
		Dissection of brain from dead person		1
		Any one ethical issue from:		
		Must not cause damage to patient's brain		
		Patients may not be able to give permission		1
19	(a)	No		0
		The best chance is at or just after 14 days.		1
		That's when the egg is released / level of LH (luteinising hormone) is at its highest.		1
	(b)	Maintains lining of uterus		1
		Inhibits both FSH and LH		1
	(c)	**Any two from:**		
		They inhibit FSH.		
		No eggs mature (and they cannot be fertilised).		
		Progesterone causes production of sticky mucus, which hinders movement of sperm.		2
	(d)	**Any two from:**		
		Success rates are not high		
		Can lead to multiple births		
		Multiple births have a risk for mother / babies		
		Very stressful		2
20		Bean plant from seed		1
21		**Any one benefit from:**		
		Produces many plants quickly		
		Rare plants can be preserved		
		All plants have desired characteristics		1
		Any one disadvantage from:		
		No genetic variation		
		All plants may be susceptible to disease / change		1
22		Select the cows and bulls that have the milk qualities required.		1
		Breed them.		1
		Select the offspring that have the best milk qualities.		1
		Repeat over a number of generations.		1
23		**Any two from:**		
		Other effects on human health not known		
		Concerns about effects on other crops		
		Concerns about effects on insects / wildlife		2

Q	Answer	Guidance	Marks
24 (a)	Allele		1
(b)	Emily and Georgina		1
25 (a)	A = 27%		1
	C + G = 46% (100 − (2 × 27) = 46%)		1
	C and G = 23% (46 ÷ 2)		1
(b)	T, T, A, G, A, T, G, T	They must all be correct for 1 mark.	1
(c)	3 amino acids		
	3 pairs of bases code for		1
	1 amino acid		
	9 base pairs = 3 sets of		1
	3 base pairs		1
26 (a)	Both parents: Ff		1
	Four offspring: FF Ff Ff ff		1
	Upper and lower case letters must be distinguishable.		1
(b)	25% or 1 in 4		1
(c)	Heterozygous		1
27 (a)	Level 3: Correct descriptions of all four control methods.		5–6
	Level 2: Correct description of control method 1 **and** one other control method (2, 3 or 4).	Allow 3 marks for a full description of methods 3 and 4 only.	3–4
	Level 1: One correct description of any control method.		1–2
	No relevant content		0

Indicative content

Control method 1
Pancreas monitors glucose level
Pancreas produces insulin if glucose level high
Glucose converted to glycogen
Glycogen stored in liver / cells

Control method 2
Pancreas produces glucagon if glucose level low
Glycogen converted to glucose by glucagon

Control method 3
Type 1: blood glucose levels tested regularly
Insulin injections if glucose level high

Control method 4
Type 2: diet control
Regular exercise

Q	Answer	Marks
(b)	**Any two from:** They: filter the blood / remove water from the blood / remove ions from the blood / reabsorb glucose into the blood / reabsorb water into the blood / reabsorb ions into the blood.	2
(c)	Proteins broken down to amino acids.	1
	Excess amino acids form ammonia (in liver).	1
	(Toxic) ammonia converted to urea.	1
	Urea removed by kidneys / less protein – less urea.	1
28	Burning trees produces more carbon dioxide in the air. / Less photosynthesis means more carbon dioxide in the air.	1
	Carbon dioxide is a greenhouse gas / causes global warming.	1
29	**Any two from:** Stabilises ecosystems / Preserves food chains / Preserves possible future crops / Preserves possible future medicines / Preserves interdependence of species	2
30	**Any one from:** Maintains the ability to produce indefinitely / Does not damage the Earth for future generations / Can carry on forever	1